Canons
and Commentaries
on Marriage

Canons and Commentaries on Marriage

Ignatius Gramunt
Javier Hervada
LeRoy A. Wauck

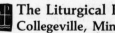 The Liturgical Press
Collegeville, Minnesota

Cover design by Don Molloy.

9   8   7   6   5   4   3   2   1

Library of Congress Cataloging-in-Publication Data
Gramunt, Ignatius, 1932-
    Canons and commentaries on marriage.
    Includes index.
    1. Marriage (Canon law)   I. Hervada, Javier,
1934—   II. Wauck, LeRoy A. III. Title.
LAW   262.9′4   87-4204
ISBN 0-8146-1552-X

CONTENTS

PART III

Marriage Nullity on Grounds of Consensual Incapacity
Canon 1095 and Its Application by Judicial Process
Rev. Ignatius Gramunt
Prof. Leroy A. Wauck

FOREWORD

In the short time that has elapsed since the close of Vatican Council II, the theology, the liturgy, and the canon law of matrimony have developed considerably. Perhaps nowhere else is the sacred and stable nature of marriage more clearly and comprehensively stated than in the crisp formulas of the new Code of Canon Law, in effect since November 27, 1983.

Canons and Commentaries on Marriage is a masterful volume because it goes directly to the basics of the Catholic understanding of this great sacrament, "the intimate partnership of life and love, established by the Creator and qualified by his laws." (*Gaudium et Spes,* n. 48) The authors give a very clear and concise account of how the Church goes about its sacred trust of teaching, celebrating, upholding the sacrament, safeguarding its holiness and dignity through her substantive law, safeguarding the individual's right to marriage through her procedural law.

If a personal note is permitted, I would point out that Part III of this volume on consensual incapacity is a happy reminder of how this fast-developing jurisprudence, supported now by the new C 1095, has greatly matured since my days as a young canonist delving into the matter while the sessions of Vatican II were in progress. There is no doubt about it—one of the surest signs of genuine Church renewal in the wake of Vatican Council II is the emergence of solid scholarship, exemplified in this volume, regarding the marvel and mystery called marriage.

Most Rev. John R. Keating
Bishop of Arlington

PART I

MATRIMONIAL LAW

Commentaries on Canons 1055-1165

Prof. Javier Hervada, J.D., J.C.D.
University of Navarre, Pamplona, Spain

1

NATURE OF MARRIAGE

(Code of Canon Law, Book IV, Title VII; CC 1055–1062)

Covenant and Sacrament

C 1055

§1. The matrimonial covenant, by which a man and a woman establish between themselves a partnership of the whole of life, is by its nature ordered toward the good of the spouses and the procreation and education of offspring; this covenant between baptized persons has been raised by Christ the Lord to the dignity of a sacrament.

§2. For this reason a matrimonial contract cannot validly exist between baptized persons unless it is also a sacrament by that fact.

This canon contains the following *doctrinal principles* concerning marriage: (1) marriage between baptized persons is a *sacrament,* (2) the sign of the sacrament is a *covenant* or contract of a special nature, (3) the object of the covenant, or that which is contracted, is a special *partnership* which involves the entire life of the contracting parties, (4) the end or purpose of this partnership of life is the common good of the spouses who enter into this special companionship for the procreation and education of offspring.

The words of the canon are taken almost literally from the Constitution *Gaudium et Spes,* n. 48, of the Second Vatican Council:

The intimate partnership of life and love which constitutes the married state has been established by the Creator and endowed by him with its proper laws; it is rooted in the contract of partners, i.e., in their irrevocable consent. . . . By its very nature the institution of marriage and married love is ordered to the procreation and education of offspring, and it is in them that it finds its crowning glory. Thus, the man and woman who "are no longer two but one" (Matt 19:6) help and serve each other by their marriage partnership . . . (and) our Savior, the Spouse of the Church, now encounters Christian spouses through the sacrament of marriage.

In order to emphasize the union between covenant and sacrament, the second paragraph of this canon states that between the baptized, there cannot be a *valid* matrimonial contract that is not at the same time a sacrament. Therefore, there is no such thing as a merely "natural" marriage between the baptized, for if the contract is by law invalid, there is no marriage but an "unlawful union" (cf. [2] of our commentary to C 1100).

Essential Properties of Marriage

C 1056

The essential properties of marriage are unity and indissolubility, which in Christian marriage obtain a special firmness in virtue of the sacrament.

Two *essential properties* characterize the special partnership or bond that originates from the marriage covenant; *unity* and *indissolubility*. These properties are required by natural law and are present in every valid marriage, even that contracted by non-Christians. According to the teaching contained in *Gaudium et Spes*, n. 48, these properties are required by "the intimate union of marriage as a mutual giving of two persons, and by the good of the children (which) demands total fidelity from the spouses and requires an unbreakable unity between them." These properties are particularly strengthened by the grace of the sacrament, which provides a specific aid to the spouses to remain indissolubly faithful to each other.

Since unity and indissolubility are *essential* properties, to exclude them in the marriage contract renders the marriage covenant invalid. For the same reason, civil divorce cannot dissolve the marriage bond, and a divorced person cannot enter into a new valid marriage while the first spouse is still alive.

Matrimonial Consent

C 1057

§1. Marriage is brought about through the consent of the parties, legitimately manifested between persons who are capable according to law of giving consent; no human power can replace this consent.

§2. Matrimonial consent is an act of the will by which a man and a woman, through an irrevocable covenant, mutually give and accept each other in order to establish marriage.

(1) Three things must be distinguished in marriage: Its *cause*, which is the covenant or contract; its *essence*, which is the marriage bond, or irrevocable partnership of life; and its *ends*, which are procreation and education of offspring, regulation of the sexual appetite, and mutual assistance (cf. S. Th., Suppl., q. 44, a. 2 & 3).

(2) This canon deals with *consent*, the decisive element or efficient cause of the marriage covenant, which consists of an *act of the will* concerning very personal rights, such as the surrender of one's body, and which, consequently, cannot be supplied by anyone other than the persons consenting. Neither the law, the parents, nor any other authority can replace *personal* consent. Consequently, human law cannot acknowledge as valid a marriage that is null by reason of a lack of that minimal consent required by the natural law.

The *object of consent* (and the object of the covenant) is described in the second paragraph of this canon: A man and a woman give and accept themselves in their sexuality as it relates to the ends of marriage, or expressed in another way, a man and a woman give themselves as *spouses*. In the marriage covenant the woman gives herself as spouse to the man, and the man gives himself as spouse to the woman, and both accept each other as spouses.

Right to Marry

C 1058

All persons who are not prohibited by law can contract marriage.

This canon establishes the right of marriage, or *ius connubii*, as a natural right of the human person. This right includes the right to contract marriage and the right to choose one's spouse freely. As a natural right, it can be restricted only for grave and just reasons and, in accordance with C 18, the laws that restrict the free exercise of rights are to be interpreted strictly. In case of doubt, therefore, the right to marry prevails over the restrictive law.

Laws Governing Marriage

C 1059

Even if only one party is baptized, the marriage of Catholics is regulated not only by divine law but also by canon law, with due regard for the competence of civil authority concerning the merely civil effects of such a marriage.

This canon is essentially a repetition of C 1016 of the former Code. It restates the exclusive jurisdiction of the Church over canonical marriage, except for its merely civil effects, which belong to the competence of the civil authority. It raises very important questions concerning Church-State relations, for it claims the divine right of the Church over an entire matrimonial system involving the baptized, except for the so-called "merely civil effects."

Civil legislation in the United States acknowledges canonical marriage only as a particular contractual formality, but it does not acknowledge the canonical effects of a marriage contracted in the Church nor the indissolubility of any validly contracted marriage. The Church tolerates this *de facto* situation without approving it, for as the canon states, the marriage of Catholics, even when only one party is baptized, is governed by divine law and by all the requirements of canon law.

Presumption in Favor of Marriage

C 1060

Marriage enjoys the favor of the law; consequently, when a doubt exists the validity of a marriage is to be upheld until the contrary is proven.

The practical importance of this principle in the judicial decisions concerning nullity of marriage is obvious: unless otherwise proved, one must stand for the validity of the marriage being contested.

There is however an exception to this principle. In case of doubt, the "privilege of the faith" enjoys the favor of the law. This exception does not appear in our canon, which otherwise reads as C 1016 of the old Code where the exception was explicitly mentioned, but the omission does not change the principle, for it is still explicitly made in C 1150 of the present Code.

Definition of Terms: Ratum tantum, Ratum et consummatum, Putative

C 1061

§1. A valid marriage between baptized persons is called ratified only if it has not been consummated; it is called ratified and consummated if the parties have performed between themselves in a human manner the conjugal act which is per se suitable for the generation of children, to which marriage is ordered by its very nature and by which the spouses become one flesh.

§2. After marriage has been celebrated, if the spouses have cohabited consummation is presumed until the contrary is proven.

§3. An invalid marriage is called putative if it has been celebrated in good faith by at least one of the parties, until both parties become certain of its nullity.

(1) This canon is first concerned with the definition of terms: a *valid* marriage can be "merely ratified" *(ratum tantum)* and "ratified and consummated" *(ratum et consummatum)*; consummation is presumed if there has been cohabitation *after* celebration of marriage. An *invalid* marriage that is reputed valid by at least one of the parties is called *putativum*.

The distinction between *ratum tantum* and *ratum et consummatum* is of special importance as it refers to the possible dissolution of the bond of a marriage that is *ratum tantum* (contemplated by CC 1141–1142). At this moment, however, all that is needed is to clarify that this distinction applies only to *Christian marriage*. The term *ratum*, which literally means that the agreement is "ratified" or made legally valid, refers only to marriage between baptized persons, and in this sense, it means *sacramental* marriage. The marriage between non-Christians may also be consummated and non-consummated, but the Code and canonical theory are mainly concerned with the marriage that is both a contract and a sacrament.

(2) There is a significant difference between this canon and its corresponding C 1015 of the old Code: a marriage is consummated by the conjugal act *humano modo* apt for the generation of offspring. *Humano modo* here means that the act must be a human act—known and willed, and in itself apt for generation. If the conjugal act does not have these conditions there is no true rendering of one another's body, to which matrimony is ordained by its own nature and by which the spouses become one flesh.

The Promise to Marry

C 1062

§1. A promise of marriage, be it unilateral or bilateral, called an engagement, is regulated by particular law which has been established by the conference of bishops after it has taken into consideration any existing customs and civil laws.

§2. A promise to marry does not give rise to an action to seek the celebration of marriage; an action for reparation of damages, however, does arise if it is warranted.

The promise of marriage or engagement is to be ruled by particular legislation of the Episcopal Conference. In the absence of this legislation, natural law and custom must rule both the moral and legal effect of such contractual promise. Canon law recognizes no legal action to compel the celebration of marriage, but only legal action for reparation of damages resulting from breach of promise. This action can be brought before an ecclesiastical court or a civil court. In any case, the suit for damages has no legal force to stop the marriage of the defendant with a third party.

2

PREPARATIONS FOR MARRIAGE*

(Code of Canon Law, Book IV, Title VII, Chap. I, CC 1063–1072)

Pastoral Care of Marriage

C 1063

Pastors of souls are obliged to see to it that their own ecclesial community furnishes the Christian faithful assistance so that the matrimonial state is maintained in a Christian spirit and makes progress toward perfection. This assistance is especially to be furnished through

1° preaching catechesis adapted to minors, youths and adults, and even the use of the media of social communications so that through these means the Christian faithful may be instructed concerning the meaning of Christian marriage and the duty of Christian spouses and parents;

2° personal preparation for entering marriage so that through such preparation the parties may be predisposed toward the holiness and duties of their new state;

3° a fruitful liturgical celebration of marriage clarifying that the spouses signify and share in that mystery of unity and of fruitful love that exists between Christ and the Church;

4° assistance furnished to those already married so that, while faithfully maintaining and protecting the conjugal covenant, they may day by day come to lead holier and fuller lives in their families.

---

*The commentaries to CC 1063–1694 substantially follow Dr. J. Forne's commentaries in *Código de Derecho Canónico*, EUNSA, Pamplona (Spain), 1983.

C 1064

It is up to the local ordinary to make provisions that such assistance is duly organized, even after consulting men and women of proven experience and skill, if it seems appropriate.

These canons, which greatly expand the pastoral care prescribed by the former Code, reflect the teaching of the Second Vatican Council on marriage as a way to holiness (cf. *Lumen Gentium*, n. 41 and *Gaudium et Spes*, nn. 47–52). The same teaching is contained in subsequent pontifical documents and mainly in the Apostolic Exhortation *Familiaris Consortio* of John Paul II. This document, furthermore, expounds at length the four pastoral stages listed in C 1063. These stages are (1) a remote and general catechesis, (2) a proximate instruction of the couple to be married, (3) a marriage catechesis within the liturgical celebration of marriage, and (4) a continuing pastoral care of those who have entered marriage.

It belongs to the bishop, in the first place, to promote this pastoral care in all its stages. Others entrusted with the care of souls must seek to involve the entire ecclesial community in this pastoral care, including, if necessary, the aid of lay men and women of experience and proven competence.

Concerning the instruction of the couple, or second stage of this pastoral care, the following should be noted:

(1) The obligation to instruct falls mainly upon the pastor of souls but should not be made strictly mandatory for the couple: "Without underestimating the necessity and obligation of the immediate preparation for marriage, which would be the case if dispensations from it were to be easily given, such preparation should be planned and practiced in such a way that its omission would not be an impediment to the celebration of marriage" (cf. John Paul II, *Familiaris Consortio*, n. 66). Pastors should be sensitive to the *ius connubii* stated in C 1058; they should be aware of the principle that only the Supreme Authority can establish impediments to marriage (cf. C 1075) and that neither the ordinary nor local custom have such power (cf. CC 1076 and 1077). The pastor, therefore, must keep a prudent balance between need for appropriate personal instruction before marriage, as prescribed in C 1063, and the *ius connubii* which he has no authority to restrict in actual practice.

(2) This instruction should not be confused with the investigation prescribed by C 1066.

The third stage, or marriage catechesis within the liturgical celebration, is also prescribed by the Order for Celebrating Marriage (S.C. of Rites, March 19, 1969).

C 1065

§1. If they can do so without serious inconvenience, Catholics who have not yet received the sacrament of confirmation are to receive it before being admitted to marriage.

§2. It is strongly recommended that those to be married approach the sacraments of penance and the Most Holy Eucharist so that they may fruitfully receive the sacrament of marriage.

The personal instruction prescribed in the two preceding canons will be most effective if it is joined with the encouragement to receive the sacraments of confirmation (if needed), penance, and Holy Communion for which appropriate but simple instruction may also be required.

Investigations Preceding Marriage

C 1066

Before marriage is celebrated, it must be evident that nothing stands in the way of its valid and licit celebration.

C 1067

The conference of bishops is to issue norms concerning the examination of the parties, and the marriage banns or other appropriate means for carrying out the necessary inquiries which are to precede marriage. The pastor can proceed to assist at a marriage after such norms have been diligently observed.

(1) C 1066 states the general principle that, before the celebration of marriage, it must be established that nothing stands in the way of this celebration being valid and licit. C 1067 leaves to the Episcopal Conference the determination of procedures to acquire this certainty, and points out three lines of investigation: (a) personal examination of the parties, (b) publication of banns, and (c) other appropriate means of inquiry. In the absence of further determination of procedures by the Episcopal Conference, the norms existing in each diocese prevail.

(2) The *personal examination* of the parties should not be confused with that *personal preparation* prescribed by C 1063, n. 3. The *personal examination* is an investigative procedure concerning possible obstacles to marriage and should not be omitted. The *personal preparation* is a pastoral instruction to dispose the spouses to the holiness and obligations of marriage (cf. C 1063, n. 2) and can only be dispensed for sound pastoral reasons, as explained before.

There is no mention in these canons of the certificate of baptism prescribed by C 1021 of the old Code, but this omission should not be interpreted as a derogation of this procedural requirement, for this and other procedural requirements fall now under particular legislation of the Episcopal Conference and need not be included in the general legislation of the Code. A certificate of baptism issued within the last six months remains as a proof of a person's freedom to marry.

(3) It should also be noted that the obligation of assuring that no obstacles stand in the way of the marriage falls (a) upon the pastor, who must conduct the investigation by himself or through others (cf. C 1070), and (b) upon the person who, empowered with due delegation, assists at the marriage (cf. C 1114 and commentary).

C 1068

Unless contrary indications are present, in danger of death, if other means of proof cannot be obtained, it is sufficient that the parties affirm—even under oath, if the case warrants it—that they have been baptized and that they are not held back by any impediment.

Here it should be noted that this abbreviated procedure cannot be extended to cases other than those of danger of death, as explicitly stated in this canon (cf. *Acta Apostolicae Sedis* 12 [1921] 349).

C 1069

All the faithful are obliged to reveal any impediments they are aware of to the pastor or to the local ordinary before the celebration of marriage.

This canon contains a partial application of that general obligation that falls upon all the faithful to care for the sanctity of marriage and protect it from possible abuses (cf. C 1063). But in order to fulfill this obligation, Catholics must be properly instructed about the nature of marriage, its essential properties, and the main laws governing it. This is even more urgent when false opinions concerning marriage are widespread in society and have entered into the Catholic community. Hence, pastors of souls must be solicitous for the general catechesis mentioned in C 1063, n. 1.

C 1070

If someone other than the pastor who is to assist at the marriage has conducted the investigations, that person is to notify the pastor of the results as soon as possible through an authentic document.

"Authentic" document here means that the document must be drawn or ordered to be drawn by the person who has conducted the investigations; the document should not be spurious, or originated by someone else. It is not enough to notify the results of the investigation to the pastor; this information should be supported by the testimony of the investigator, who should take responsibility for it. In practice this is done by signing the forms which the chancery office provides for the documentation of these investigations.

Celebrations Requiring Permission of the Local Ordinary

C 1071

§1. Except in case of necessity, no one is to assist at the following marriages without the permission of the local ordinary:

1° the marriage of transients;

2° a marriage which cannot be recognized or celebrated in accord with the norm of civil law;

3° a marriage of a person who is bound by natural obligations toward another party or toward children, arising from a prior union;

4° a marriage of a person who has notoriously rejected the Catholic faith;

5° a marriage of a person who is bound by a censure;

6° a marriage of a minor child when the parents are unaware of it or are reasonably opposed to it;

7° a marriage to be entered by means of a proxy, mentioned in can. 1105.

§2. The local ordinary is not to grant permission for assisting at the marriage of a person who has notoriously rejected the Catholic faith unless the norms of can. 1125 have been observed, making any necessary adaptations.

This canon lists a number of situations which may contain some obstacles to the valid or licit celebration of marriage or which may give rise to legal complications.

(1) According to the definition of C 100, *vagi* or transients are those persons who have neither domicile nor quasi-domicile. All that is needed to acquire quasi-domicile for legal effects is the *intention* of residing, or *the fact* of having resided, within a given diocese for three months. If one of the parties intending to be married has no fixed residence, the matter must be referred to the ordinary who will decide how to conduct the investigation concerning the freedom from obstacles to enter a valid and licit marriage, such as, locations where banns are to be published, means of publication, affidavits from friends and relatives, declaration under oath from the person intending marriage, etc.

(2) A civil obstacle for the celebration of marriage could be insufficient age, if the minimal age required by civil law is higher than the fourteen years of age for the woman and sixteen for the man required by canon law (cf. C 1083). Another obstacle would exist if the person

intending to marry is still bound by a civil marriage, even if this marriage may not be considered valid by the law of the Church.

(3) The natural obligations mentioned in n. 3 refer only to those that could render the new marriage invalid or illicit, or give rise to important legal complications: a widow or widower with children has of course natural obligation towards the children of her or his previous marriage, but these obligations do not constitute a legal obstacle for the new marriage, and are not the kind of natural obligations contemplated by the canon. But if one of the parties intending to celebrate canonical marriage has entered a previous invalid marriage or had in fact lived in concubinage, and had contracted natural obligations towards another party or the children born from the previous union, it should be ascertained that these obligations do not represent a legal threat to the new marriage. If there is a reasonable doubt about it, the bishop should be consulted.

When a previous marriage has existed, even if the marriage was invalid in the eyes of the Church, most dioceses require that the civil decree of divorce be presented for review to the competent diocesan office as evidence that there is no obstacle for the celebration of marriage.

(4) The case mentioned in n. 4 and again covered in §2 of this canon, deserves special attention:

(a) Defection from the Catholic faith is said to be *formal* when a person baptized in the Catholic faith, knowingly and willingly, joins another religion or explicitly and externally rejects the faith or authority of the Church. A *practical* but not formal defection exists when a person does not practice the faith or behaves in a manner that conflicts with Catholic teaching. Defection, whether formal or practical, is notorious if the fact is well known in the community; it cannot be called notorious if it is known only within a limited circle of family and friends.

(b) If the defection is *formal*, whether notorious or not, this constitutes a case of mixed marriage which is forbidden by law; this prohibition, however, can be dispensed by the bishop for "just and reasonable cause" (cf. CC 1124–1125 and commentaries). If the defection is *practical* and *notorious*, the matter must be referred to the bishop; the bishop can grant permission for the celebration of the marriage, but in order to do so he must have assurance that the conditions prescribed by C 1125 have been fulfilled. These conditions are: (1) declaration of the Catholic party to avoid anything contrary to his or her faith, (2) promises of the same Catholic party to raise the children in the Catholic Church, (3) evidence that the other party has been properly informed about these promises, and (4) instruction of both parties about the ends and the essential properties of marriage.

(c) When the defection is practical and not notorious as it may often happen with Catholics who do not practice their faith, or whose behavior is in conflict with Catholic teaching, but wish to be married in the Church, the celebration of marriage cannot be forbidden (see commentary to CC 1063 and 1064). In cases of weak faith and lack of religious practices, the pastoral guidelines contained in the Apostolic Exhortation *Familiaris Consortio* of John Paul II, n. 68, should be carefully studied and applied. The pastor should take into account that the minimum required for valid and licit marriage is the "right intention . . . to consent, at least implicitly, to what the Church intends to do by the celebration of marriage." With this in mind, the pastor should try to revive the faith of the contracting parties instructing and encouraging them towards the fruitful reception of the sacraments as indicated in CC 1063 and 1065. As expressed by *Familiaris Consortio*, n. 68, "to attempt to lay down further criteria for admission to marriage concerning the level of faith of those to be married, would involve grave risks: first, the risk of unfounded and discriminatory judgments; second, the risk of causing doubts about the validity of marriages already celebrated."

(5) Concerning the situation listed in n. 5 of C 1071, those subject to excommunication or interdict are barred from the sacraments (cf. CC 1331 and 1332) and their marriage cannot be celebrated without previous recourse to the bishop. If the penalty can be absolved by the confessor in accordance with C 1357 and is in fact absolved with adherence to the provisions of this canon, the permission from the bishop to assist at this marriage is no longer required.

(6) For cases listed in n. 6, a minor is a person who is less than eighteen years old (cf. C 97).

(7) For marriages by proxy, as listed in n. 7, the permission of the bishop is required so that all legal requirements demanded in these special cases (cf. C 1105) are carefully fulfilled.

It should be observed that assisting at these marriages without previous permission of the bishop is illicit, but does not necessarily render the marriage invalid. In fact, as the canon explicitly states, permission from the bishop is not required if there is a case of necessity, that is to say, when fulfillment of this requirement would cause greater harm than its omission.

Marriage Before "Customary Age"

C 1072

Pastors of souls are to take care to prevent youths from celebrating marriage

before the age at which marriage is usually contracted in accord with the accepted practice of the region.

This canon contains a pastoral rule addressed to pastors of souls to *dissuade* from marriage those who may be too young to undertake the responsibilities of married life. The law however, does not give to pastors of souls the authority to forbid these marriages. Prohibition to marry by reason of insufficient age is limited to (1) those without the minimum age for a *valid* marriage which, as established by C 1083 is the age of sixteen for the man and fourteen for the woman; the Episcopal Conference can raise these ages but only as a requirement for *licitness;* (2) those minors who intend to contract marriage without the knowledge of their parents or against their consent (cf. C 1071, §1, no. 6).

The canon we are now studying refers to those persons who are of sufficient legal age to enter a valid marriage, have the permission of their parents if they are minors, but who have not yet reached that maturity of age necessary, by common opinion in a particular region, to undertake the responsibility of married life. Pastors should not disregard this common opinion, but should also uphold the right to marriage as defined by law. If the couple persists in their intent to marry, and there is no legal obstacle, they must be allowed to celebrate their marriage.

3

IMPEDIMENTS IN GENERAL

(Code of Canon Law, Book IV, Title VII, Chap. II, CC 1073–1082)

Diriment Impediments

The old Code followed the classic distinction between *diriment* impediments, which made a person incapable of entering a *valid* marriage, and *prohibitive* impediments which simply forbade a person to be married, but did not render the marriage invalid if celebrated against the prohibitive law.

In the new Code there are no prohibitive impediments and, although certain prohibitions remain which would make a marriage illicit but valid, these prohibitions do not receive the name of impediments in the strictest sense. The only impediments that remain are those called *diriment,* a term maintained by the new Code even if the former distinction is not explicitly used. Before treating of each impediment in particular, some general principles on impediments and their dispensation are covered by the canons that follow:

C 1073

A diriment impediment renders a person incapable of contracting marriage validly.

The definition of impediment, or diriment impediment, is given in this canon: it consists of an incapacity for valid marriage.

17

C 1074

An impediment which can be proven in the external forum is considered to be a public impediment, otherwise it is an occult impediment.

The terms "public" and "hidden" (occult) are here defined legally. If the impediment can be proven by legal means (for example, a public record; two witnesses), it is "public," even if not publicized. If it cannot be proven by legal means, the impediment is "hidden." The distinction is important when it comes to seeking dispensation from impediments (cf. C 1079 and commentary, C 1080, C 1082).

Declaration and Enactment of Impediments

C 1075

§1. The supreme authority of the Church alone has the competency to declare authentically when divine law prohibits or voids a marriage.

§2. Only the supreme authority has the right to establish other impediments for the baptized.

C 1076

A custom which introduces a new impediment or which is contrary to existing impediments is reprobated.

C 1075 distinguishes between impediments of *divine law* and impediments of *ecclesiastical law*. The impediments of divine law are *established* by natural or by divine-positive law but are *declared* as such only by the supreme authority; impediments of *ecclesiastical law* can be established by the supreme authority alone and only upon the baptized. Any restriction of the *ius connubii* (cf. C 1058), is therefore, exclusively reserved to the Roman Pontiff and to the Episcopal College (cf. C 331 and C 326). The diocesan bishop has no power to introduce any new impediments nor can any custom introduce a practice contrary to the general law (cf. C 1076). As canonical theory has always emphasized, impediments to marriage must be regarded as exceptional, they must be explicitly established by law, and they must be strictly interpreted (cf. C 18).

C 1077

§1. In a particular case the local ordinary can prohibit the marriage of his own subjects wherever they are staying and of all persons actually present in his own territory, but only for a time, for a serious cause and as long as that cause exists.

§2. Only the supreme authority of the Church can add an invalidating clause to a prohibition.

The limits of the power of local ordinaries to restrict the right to marriage are here more closely determined: (1) the prohibition must be addressed in individual cases, not to general situations, (2) it can reach those residing in his territory and those who remain under his authority even if they reside outside his territory, (3) it cannot be a prohibition in perpetuity, but it can be given for as long as the cause continues, (4) there must be a grave cause, as would be the case if the celebration of marriage would cause grave scandal among the faithful, and (5) this prohibition can never have a diriment character: if the marriage was celebrated against the decree of the bishop, the marriage would be valid.

When a marriage has been declared null by judicial decision, the court or the ordinary may forbid the celebration of a new marriage (cf. CC 1684 and 1685) but this prohibition is subject to the restrictions of this canon.

Dispensation from Impediments

C 1078

§1. The local ordinary can dispense his own subjects wherever they are staying as well as all persons actually present in his own territory from all the impediments of ecclesiastical law with the exception of those impediments whose dispensation is reserved to the Apostolic See.

§2. A dispensation from the following impediments is reserved to the Apostolic See:

1° the impediment arising from sacred orders or from a public perpetual vow of chastity in a religious institute of pontifical right;

2° the impediment of crime mentioned in can. 1090.

§3. A dispensation is never given from the impediment of consanguinity in the direct line or in the second degree of the collateral line.

(1) According to C 85, a *dispensation* is a "relaxation of a merely ecclesiastical law in a particular case." Only the *ecclesiastical law* can be relaxed by human ecclesiastical authority; divine law, whether natural or positive, is beyond the power of the human authority and is not subject to dispensation. Consequently, no dispensation can be granted from impediments of natural law and divine-positive law.

In *normal circumstances*, matrimonial impediments deriving from ecclesiastical law can be dispensed only by the local ordinary and by the Holy See. Under the term local ordinary are included the diocesan bishop, the vicar general, and the episcopal vicars (cf. C 134). The local ordinary dispenses from all ecclesiastical law impediments not reserved to the Holy See. It is understood, of course, that no one should licitly dispense from the precepts of the law unless there is just and reasonable cause (cf. C 90).

(2) Concerning the impediments reserved to the Holy See, which are mentioned in the second paragraph of this canon, it should be noted that within the impediment of sacred orders, the diaconate, whether temporal or permanent, is included.

(3) The third paragraph of this canon deserves special commentary, for the computation of degrees of consanguinity in the collateral line is not to be done according to the former Code, which followed a system derived from Germanic law, but in accordance with C 108 of the new Code, which adopts the Roman law tradition. Consanguinity can be defined as family relationship derived from generation. This relation exists in the *direct line* of descent (grandparents, parents, children, grandchildren, etc.) and in the *collateral line* (mothers and sisters; uncles, aunts, nephews and nieces, cousins).

Family relationship is measured by degrees, which should be computed as established by C 108:

§1. Consanguinity is calculated through lines and degrees.

§2. In the direct line, there are as many degrees as there are generations or persons, not counting the common ancestor.

§3. In the collateral line, there are as many degrees as there are persons in both lines together, not counting the common ancestor.

Thus, grandfather and granddaughter are related in the *direct line* of consanguinity in the second degree; brother and sister are related in the *collateral line* of consanguinity in the third degree; cousins whose fathers (or mothers) are brothers (or sisters) are related in the *collateral line* in the fourth degree.

The impediment of consanguinity is established by C 1091 and, although in the collateral line can be dispensed beyond the second degree, the canon on which we are now commenting explicitly states that no dispensation can be granted for the direct line of consanguinity in any degree, or for the collateral line in the second degree (brothers and sisters). In the direct line, the impediment is clearly one of natural law; in the collateral line, is, very probably, of natural law also and therefore not dispensible. A marriage contracted under such an impediment would always be null.

Dispensation in Emergency Cases

C 1079

§1. In danger of death, the local ordinary can dispense his own subjects wher-

ever they are staying as well as all persons who are actually present in his territory both from the form prescribed for the celebration of matrimony and from
each and every impediment of ecclesiastical law, whether it be public or occult,
except the impediment arising from sacred order of the presbyterate.

§2. In the same situation mentioned in §1 and only for cases in which the
local ordinary cannot be reached, the pastor, the properly delegated sacred minister and the priest or deacon who assists at matrimony in accord with the norm
of can. 1116, §2, also possess the faculty to dispense from the same impediments.

§3. In danger of death a confessor enjoys the faculty to dispense from occult
impediments for the internal forum, whether within or outside the act of
sacramental confession.

§4. In the case mentioned in §2, the local ordinary is not considered to be
accessible if he can be contacted only by means of telegraph or telephone.

In the previous canon we saw who is empowered to grant dispensation
from an impediment under normal circumstances. This canon provides
for the dispensation of impediments from ecclesiastical law in *danger
of death*. In this situation the general law grants powers to dispense to
the following persons:

(1) The local ordinary, a term including the diocesan bishop, the vicar
general and the episcopal vicars (cf. C 134). The reservation of a number of impediments to the Holy See as listed in C 1078, §2 ceases in danger
of death—except for the impediment derived from the priesthood which
remains reserved. Notice however, that the impediment deriving from
diaconate is no longer reserved in these cases.

The local ordinary, furthermore, can dispense from another general
law, which is not an impediment, but still necessary for validity: this
is the canonical form prescribed by C 1108, which requires the presence
of the assistant at marriage and the two witnesses.

(2) *Pastors* and *priests* or *deacons duly delegated to assist at marriage*
(cf. CC 1111 and 1116, §2) can dispense from the same impediments
when, by reason of urgency (i.e., danger of death) it is not possible to
reach the ordinary. The danger of death need not be imminent but sufficiently urgent so that recourse to the ordinary even by telephone or telegraph, may be too onerous. For this reason, according to the fourth
paragraph of this canon and for all legal effects, telephone and telegraph
do not make access to the ordinary "possible."

Besides the power to dispense from impediments, these same persons
can dispense also from canonical form.

(3) *The confessor* has powers to dispense from all hidden impediments
of ecclesiastical law in the *internal forum only*. In danger of death, some
unknown impediments may be revealed to the confessor, either within

sacramental confession itself or in conversation with the priest outside of sacramental confession. It would seem that in this canon, *hidden* should not be understood in the sense given by C 1074 as an impediment that cannot be legally proved, but as an impediment that *de facto* is not legally known. The tenor of this canon and of C 1080 that follows support our interpretation, for the extraordinary power given to the confessor for the sake of comforting the conscience of the dying person, and which is fittingly limited to dispensing in the internal forum only, would be practically meaningless if it could apply only to impediments that cannot be legally proved. If a confessor, for instance, discovers that, in danger of death the parties wishing to be married are first cousins, the impediment of consanguinity in lateral line of the fourth degree stands in the way of a valid marriage; the existence of this impediment can easily be proved by an investigation of birth certificates, and in this sense it is a "public" impediment, even if the family relationship of the two parties is not publicly known. If we were to understand that in this canon "hidden" impediment has the meaning given by C 1074, the confessor could not dispense from the impediment of consanguinity existing between two cousins; nor could he dispense in any other case where legal proof can easily be obtained concerning impediments which are in fact publicly known. It seems to us, that this contradicts the whole intention of this canon, and consequently, we must conclude that for the confessor to dispense from impediments in the internal forum it is sufficient that the impediment not be publicly known *de facto*.

C 1080

§1. Whenever an impediment is discovered after all the wedding preparations are made and the marriage cannot be deferred without probable danger of serious harm until a dispensation can be obtained from competent authority, the following persons enjoy the faculty to dispense from all the impediments with the exception of the ones mentioned in can. 1087, §2, n. 1: the local ordinary and, as long as the case is an occult one, all persons mentioned in can. 1079, §§2 and 3, observing the conditions prescribed in that canon.

§2. This power is also operative for the convalidation of a marriage if the same danger exists in delay and there is insufficient time to have recourse to the Apostolic See, or to the local ordinary concerning impediments from which he is able to dispense.

This canon contemplates another extraordinary situation traditionally known as *casus perplexus* which consists of the following facts: (1) All is prepared for the wedding, meaning that all legal requirements of the parties has been made, the baptismal certificates and other records have been accepted, the banns have been published. (2) An impediment is subsequently discovered by the assistant at the marriage, the pastor or the ordinary. Even if others knew about it, what matters is the "discovery" of the impediment by the assistant, pastor or ordinary. (3) The marriage or the validation of a marriage contracted invalidly cannot be delayed without *great harm.*

In these situations, the law gives power to dispense to the following persons: (1) The ordinary for all ecclesiastical law impediments, except the impediment of sacred orders (which includes the diaconate) and the public vow of chastity in a religious institute of pontifical right. (2) The pastor, all assistants at marriage duly delegated (cf, CC 1111 and 1116, §2) and the confessor, but only when the case is truly hidden, that is to say, *not publicly known.* The use of terms "as long as the case is an occult one" makes it clear that the meaning that C 1074 gives to hidden or occult is not to be used in these cases. All that is required in order to dispense is that the impediment not be publicly known even if it could be proved legally. If the impediment is known to some persons but remains publicly unknown, the dispensation, can be granted. The impediments of sacred orders and public vow, which the ordinary can never dispense, can neither be dispensed by the pastor, assistants or confessor.

C 1081

The pastor or the priest or deacon mentioned in can. 1079, §2, is immediately to inform the local ordinary of a dispensation granted for the external forum; it is also to be recorded in the marriage register.

C 1082

Unless a rescript from the Penitentiary states otherwise, a dispensation from an occult impediment granted in the internal nonsacramental forum is to be recorded in a book which is to be kept in the secret archive of the curia; if the occult impediment becomes public later on, no other dispensation is necessary for the external forum.

These two canons establish the obligation to keep records of the dispensations granted. This is to be done as follows: (1) For dispensations granted in the *external forum:* The dispensation from impediments, or from canonical form in danger of death, or in *casus perplexus* should be recorded in the matrimonial record kept in the parish, and the pastor or the assistant to the marriage, who have granted the dispensations, must inform the ordinary immediately. (2) For dispensations granted in the *non-sacramental internal forum* for a hidden impediment (not publicly known): These dispensations must not be entered in the parish record, but should be recorded in a special book kept in the secret archives of the diocesan curia. If the dispensation has been obtained from the Roman Penitentiary, which is the competent office of the Roman curia for these cases, the instructions of the Penitentiary, if any, should be followed. (3) Dispensations granted in *sacramental confession* for the *internal forum* should not be recorded anywhere.

If the impediment dispensed in the *non-sacramental internal forum* becomes publicly known, no further dispensation for the external forum is required, but if the dispensation was given in *sacramental confession* in the *internal forum*, and then the impediment becomes publicly known, a new dispensation in the external forum would be required.

4

SPECIFIC IMPEDIMENTS

(Code of Canon Law, Book IV, Title VII,
Chap. III, CC 1083–1094)

Insufficient Age

C 1083

§1. A man before he has completed his sixteenth year of age, and likewise a woman before she has completed her fourteenth year of age, cannot enter a valid marriage.

§2. It is within the power of the conference of bishops to establish an older age for the licit celebration of marriage.

(1) In order to understand the *nature* of this impediment, we must distinguish between the canonical concept of impediment and the defect of consent. An impediment is a legal obstacle established by law which, in some cases, can be removed by the competent authority for a just and reasonable cause. Defect of consent is an insufficiency of the very *essence* of the matrimonial covenant, for consent cannot be supplied by anyone but the individual intending to marry (cf. C 1057, §1). Whether defect of consent is voluntary or due to an inability to consent, it is conceptually different from a matrimonial impediment.

The ability to consent to the marriage covenant is indeed dependent on proper discernment and sufficient age, but inability to consent by lack of the use of reason is treated in C 1095. The impediment of "under age" established by C 1083 refers more directly to insufficient *sexual maturity*, which is needed to accomplish the ends of matrimony. In order to assure the integrity of marriage and protect it from diverse and arbitrary judgments concerning sexual maturity, the legislator establishes minimal age requirements, generally valid in all cultures and regions, in the form of an impediment. Since the particular determination of ages sixteen and fourteen is of *ecclesiastical law*, it can be dispensed in particular cases by the ordinary if there is a just and reasonable cause (cf. C 1078).

(2) The legislator, furthermore, acknowledges that, due to regional circumstances, there might be valid reasons to raise the minimal age of marriage and grants to the Episcopal Conference the authority to do so. The norm, however, established by the Episcopal Conference cannot have a "diriment," or nullifying, character, a provision that is consistent with the principle contained in C 1077, §2, which reserves to the Holy See the power to enact nullifying impediments. In addition, the Code provides a pastoral guideline in C 1072 about dissuading from marriage those who may be considered too young. As we noted in our commentary to that canon, this rule should not be converted into a practical impediment.

Impotence

C 1084

§1. Antecedent and perpetual impotence to have intercourse, whether on the part of the man or of the woman, which is either absolute or relative, of its very nature invalidates marriage.

§2. If the impediment of impotence is doubtful, either by reason of a doubt of law or a doubt of fact, a marriage is neither to be impeded nor is it to be declared null as long as the doubt exists.

§3. Sterility neither prohibits nor invalidates marriage, with due regard for the prescription of can. 1098.

(1) "Impotence" is defined as incapacity to perform the marital act. It is "antecedent" if it existed before marriage; "perpetual" if it cannot be cured by means that are licit and not dangerous to life; it is "absolute" if it prevents a person from marital intercourse with all others, and "relative" if it prevents it only with a certain person or persons.

"Sterility" is defined as incapacity for generation due to causes other than incapacity for copulation.

(2) Impotence that is antecedent and perpetual, either absolute or relative, invalidates marriage as stated in this canon. In the last sentence of the first paragraph of this canon, "of its very nature" indicates that this is an impediment of *natural law* that cannot be dispensed. Sterility does not constitute an impediment nor does it invalidate marriage, unless it had been *deceitfully* concealed from the other party in order to

obtain consent to marry. This principle is stated in the third paragraph of this canon with its reference to C 1098.

A decree of the Sacred Congregation for the Doctrine of Faith of May 13, 1977, sheds further light on this impediment as it may refer to vasectomies and other similar conditions. Only impotence, as described above, constitutes the impediment; actual emission of semen is not required for the marriage act to be sufficient for validity of marriage. A vasectomy, therefore, whether in the man or in the woman would be considered sterility and would constitute no impediment. But a vasectomy consented to *before* marriage for the purpose of *excluding offspring*, may represent a positive act of the will to exclude one of the essential elements of marriage, thus rendering consent invalid according to C 1101, §2.

(3) The doubt concerning the existence of this impediment can be *doubt of law* or *doubt of fact*. The first exists when it is not certain that the canon establishing the impediment of impotence is applicable to a particular case or several cases of the same kind; the second exists when it is not certain that impotence, as described above, exists in fact or existed before marriage, or when it is doubtful whether the condition of impotence is perpetual or not. In either case, one must stand for the validity of marriage, for marriage enjoys the favor of the law (cf. C 1060).

Previous Matrimonial Bond

C 1085

§1. A person who is held to the bond of a prior marriage, even if it has not been consummated, invalidly attempts marriage.

§2. Even if the prior marriage is invalid or dissolved for any reason whatsoever, it is not on that account permitted to contract another before the nullity or dissolution of the prior marriage has been legitimately and certainly established.

(1) Known as the impediment of *ligamen* or previous bond, this is an impediment of *divine law:* every marriage, including non-Christian marriage, is, by natural law, one and indissoluble. These essential properties of marriage are confirmed by divine positive law (cf. Gen 2:24; Matt 19:3-9; Mark 10:2-12; Luke 16:18; 1 Cor 7:2-6, 10-11, 39-40; Eph 5:32; Rom 7:3). This impediment, therefore, cannot be dispensed.

(2) The impediment *ceases* to exist by death of one of the spouses or by those two forms of dissolution of the bond regulated by CC 1142–1150. If the previous marriage has been invalidly contracted, the impediment does not really exist, but invalidity must be proved, for marriage enjoys the favor of the law (cf. C 1060).

(3) It is not licit to contract a new marriage before having obtained legal certainty that the previous bond has been dissolved or declared null. This *legal certainty* consists of the following:

(a) If the previous matrimonial bond was dissolved by the death of one's spouse, legal proof of death must be supplied. If the legal proof cannot be obtained, the diocesan bishop must issue a declaration of presumed death (cf. Part II, Chapter 18).

(b) If it is to be dissolved by the *privilege of the faith*, legal proof of the interrogation and its result must be presented (cf. C 1145 and commentary).

(c) If the previous bond was dissolved by dispensation of *ratum et non-consummatum*, proof of the dispensation by the Roman Pontiff must be obtained (cf. Part II, Chapter 17).

(d) If the previous marriage had been invalidly contracted because of *defect of consent, defect of form,* or by reason of a diriment *impediment,* judicial sentence must first be obtained (cf. Part II, Chapters 14 and 15).

Disparity of Cult

C 1086

§1. Marriage between two persons, one of whom is baptized in the Catholic Church or has been received into it and has not left it by means of a formal act, and the other of whom is non-baptized, is invalid.

§2. This impediment is not to be dispensed unless the conditions mentioned in cann. 1125 and 1126 are fulfilled.

§3. If at the time the marriage was contracted one party was commonly considered to be baptized or the person's baptism was doubted, the validity of the marriage is to be presumed in accord with the norm of can. 1060 until it is proven with certainty that one party was baptized and the other was not.

This is the impediment known as disparity of cult (difference of religion or worship) which exists when one of the parties intending marriage is a Catholic and the other a non-Christian. This situation must not be confused with the so called "mixed marriage" contemplated by CC 1124–1129, where one party is a baptized Catholic and the other a person baptized in a non-Catholic community.

The reason for this impediment is the following: a baptized Catholic is a person who, having received the gift of faith in Jesus Christ, becomes one of Christ's faithful and part of a "chosen race," a "holy nation," a "people that belong to God" (cf. 1 Pet 2:9-10). By *divine law,* therefore, a Christian has the right and obligation to nourish and protect this incomparable gift and not expose it to being lost or diminished. A close association and intimate communion of life with someone who does not share the faith can exercise a deleterious influence on the gift of faith.

For these reasons, the legislator established an impediment as a general law for the sake of the common good, even if in actual fact, the marriage of a Catholic with a non-Christian may not represent a danger to the faith. In this sense, it is an impediment of *ecclesiastical law* that can be dispensed. This impediment is regulated by the canon as follows:

(1) *One of the parties must be a Catholic.* A person becomes a Catholic by baptism in the Catholic Church or by valid baptism in a non-Catholic community and later reception into the Catholic Church.

(2) It does not affect the person who has *defected by formal act* from the Catholic Church. A *formal act* of defection, as we have seen in our commentary to C 1071, §4, must be interpreted strictly. A non-practicing Catholic even if notoriously known as not practicing, has not *formally* defected. A formal defection exists by the act of apostasy, heresy, or schism externally manifested. Such a formal act of defection would bring about an excommunication and a prohibition against being married in the Church. As far as the impediment, C 1086 determines that it would not apply to the person who has formally defected. Therefore, if this person contracts marriage with a non-baptized person, the marriage is valid.

(3) The other party must be a *non-baptized* person. In the case of some persons raised in Protestant communities which do not baptize infants or where there is doubt about the validity of their baptism, investigation about the existence of valid baptism should be made, for if it turns out that the person has been validly baptized, this impediment does not exist, although the marriage would still be illicit and the provisions of CC 1124–1129 for "mixed marriages" should be observed. It should also be noted in this regard that baptism by "aspersion" or sprinkling is not considered valid (cf. C 854).

If the marriage has taken place and doubt arises about the existence or validity of baptism, matrimony enjoys the favor of the law and the marriage is considered valid until otherwise proved in accordance with C 1060.

(4) This impediment can be dispensed by the ordinary as established in C 1078 if the following conditions are fulfilled: (a) the Catholic party is to declare his or her intention to remove the danger of defecting from the faith, (b) the same party should promise to do all in his or her power to baptize and raise the children in the Catholic faith, (c) the non-Catholic party should be made aware of these promises and obligations of the Catholic party, and (d) both parties are to be instructed about the purposes and essential properties of marriage (cf. C 1125).

Sacred Orders

C 1087

Persons who are in holy orders invalidly attempt marriage.

(1) This is an impediment of *ecclesiastical law* which can be dispensed, but only by the Roman Pontiff. Although celibacy is not an essential requirement of the priesthood, it is however solidly grounded in Holy Scripture (cf. Matt 19:12; Luke 18:28-30; 1 Cor 7:5, 32-34, etc.) and in a long ecclesiastical tradition recently confirmed by the Magisterium (cf. Vatican II, *Lumen Gentium*, n. 29; *Presbyterorum ordinis*, n. 16; *Optatum Optius*, n. 10; Paul VI, Encyclical *Sacerdotalis caelibatus;* John Paul II, Letter to priests, *Novo Suscipiente*, of April 8, 1979).

This impediment obviously affects all those who have *validly* received holy orders: episcopate, presbyterate, diaconate. It affects, therefore, the permanent deacon who becomes a widower and it extends to those who have lost the clerical state by penalty or by rescript of the Holy See, since loss of the clerical state does not carry dispensation from celibacy unless the ordination has been declared invalid (cf. CC 290 and 291).

(2) The dispensation from this impediment belongs exclusively to the Roman Pontiff, as we have seen in C 1075. To request this dispensation, the *Norms* of the Sacred Congregation for the Doctrine of the Faith (October 14, 1980) should be followed.

(3) The attempt to marry, even civilly, under this impediment carries removal from ecclesiastical office (cf. C 194) and suspension *latae sententiae*, and if after proper admonition the cleric does not reform, he can be punished with other penalties and with dismissal from the clerical state (cf. 1394).

Public Perpetual Vow of Chastity

C 1088

Persons who are bound by a public perpetual vow of chastity in a religious institute invalidly attempt marriage.

(1) A vow is a free and deliberate promise made to God which must be observed in conscience by force of the virtue of religion, and a vow of perfect chastity is obviously opposed to matrimony and its essential obligation of rendering the marital debt. To enter into the matrimonial contract while the vow of chastity is still in force would violate the vow, it would be a grave sin, and it would be therefore, illicit. In this sense, the root of this impediment is of *divine law*.

Such a vow, however, would not by itself make the matrimonial contract invalid, unless the legislator, for the sake of the common good, determines otherwise by means of a nullifying impediment arising from the vow itself. In this sense, this nullifying impediment is one of *ecclesiastical law*.

(2) The present Code has considerably simplified this impediment compared to the former Code. A public and perpetual vow of chastity in a religious institute is now the only cause of this impediment. More precisely, the impediment arises: (a) From a *vow* of chastity, not from a *promise* or from any other bond or manner of consecration to God; (b) given in a *religious* institute (cf. C 607), not in a *secular* institute (cf. C 712) or in a society of apostolic life (cf. CC 731 and 732); (c) must be a "public" vow, that is to say, a vow received in the name of the Church by the legitimate superior (cf. C 1192); (d) must be *perpetual*, thus excluding other public but temporary vows of chastity (cf. CC 654–658).

(3) This impediment *ceases* to exist with the indult to leave the religious institute. Petition for the indult must be presented to the superior general of the institute who will evaluate it, and forward it to the competent ecclesiastical authority. For religious institutes of pontifical right, the competent authority to grant the indult is the Holy See; for institutes of diocesan right, the competent authority is the diocesan bishop (cf. C 691).

If the religious asking for the indult is someone who has received Holy Orders, the *Norms* of the Sacred Congregation for the Doctrine of the Faith of October 14, 1980, must be observed.

(4) The religious who attempts marriage, even civil marriage, is summarily dismissed from the religious institute, and if he is a cleric, falls into suspension *latae sententiae;* if not a cleric, he or she falls into interdict *latae sententiae* (cf. CC 694 and 1394).

Abduction

C 1089

No marriage can exist between a man and a woman abducted or at least detained for the purpose of contracting marriage with her, unless the woman of her own accord chooses marriage after she has been separated from her abductor and established in a place where she is safe and free.

(1) This is known as the impediment of abduction. Although based upon the requirement of natural law that a person must be free to give valid matrimonial consent, the specific configuration of this impediment is of ecclesiastical law. For the sake of the common good, and without enter-

ing into deeper questions regarding free consent which are the subject-matter of the following chapter in the new Code, the legislator has established that certain external acts of abduction constitute an impediment that render matrimony invalid. In the new Code, however, this impediment has been greatly simplified. Its legal configuration is as follows: (a) the abductor must be the man, not the woman, (b) the abduction can take the form of *carrying off* the woman by force or fraud, or forcefully *retaining* her in one place, and (c) there must be an intention of marrying her, either before or after the act of abduction has taken place.

(2) The impediment *ceases:* (a) by separation of the woman from her abductor *and* (b) by establishing the woman in a safe and free place. The moment these two conditions are fulfilled, the impediment ceases to exist. There might still be a question about her freedom to marry, and this indeed must be examined for matrimonial consent to be valid, but the legal impediment no longer exists and no dispensation is required. It would not be logical, therefore, to request or grant a dispensation from this impediment when it can cease to exist by fulfilling the two conditions stated.

(3) It should be noted that abduction is also a canonical crime (cf. C 1397) that should be punished with certain privations and prohibitions as listed in C 1336, even if the impediment has ceased to exist.

Crime

C 1090

§1. A person who for the purpose of entering marriage with a certain person has brought about the death of that person's spouse or one's own spouse, invalidly attempts such a marriage.

§2. They also invalidly attempt marriage between themselves who have brought about the death of the spouse of one of them through mutual physical or moral cooperation.

(1) This impediment, known as impediment of crime, or *crimen,* has been considerably simplified in the new Code. Now, the impediment arises from the following situations: (a) Causing the death of one's spouse; (b) causing the death of the spouse of the person one intends to marry; (c) cooperation in causing the death of either's spouse.

(2) The legal configuration of this impediment requires: (a) that either one of the parties has caused the death of either's spouse directly or through a third person; (b) that the death of the spouse has really occurred (the failed attempt to kill the spouse would not give rise to the

impediment); (c) that the crime was perpetrated with the intention of marrying a specific person. The intention of killing in order to be free to marry someone in general would not cause the impediment.

(3) The *dispensation* of this impediment is *reserved* to the Roman Pontiff (C 1078).

Since homicide is also a canonical crime, consideration should be given to certain canonical penalties as prescribed by C 1397.

Consanguinity

C 1091

§1. In the direct line of consanguinity, marriage is invalid between all ancestors and descendants, whether they be related legitimately or naturally.

§2. In the collateral line of consanguinity, marriage is invalid up to and including the fourth degree.

§3. The impediment of consanguinity is not multiplied.

§4. If there exists any doubt whether the parties are related through consanguinity in any degree of the direct line or in the second degree of the collateral line, marriage is never permitted.

(1) This and the following canons establish four impediments originating from *family relationships*. The purpose of these impediments is to protect the spiritual integrity of family relations against their possible degeneration into sexual relations with the hope of future marriage among family members. Some of these impediments are of *divine law*, as is most certain the case among parents and children, and very probably between direct-line descendants and ascendants and between brothers and sisters.

The concrete determination of the natural law impediment to other family relations is of *ecclesiastical law*, for it depends on social and cultural circumstances. As the nuclear family becomes more mobile, and the actual relationships between relatives more confined to the members of the nuclear family, these impediments tend to affect fewer people. This explains why the new Code retains those impediments between closer relatives while suppressing the impediment of spiritual relationship and affinity in the lateral line of the former Code.

(2) There is another important change in the new Code: As explained in our commentary to C 1078, the computation of degrees must be done according to the reckoning established by CC 108 and 109, which adopt the Roman law tradition.

(3) *Consanguinity* is that family relationship that originates from generation. This impediment is regulated as follows: (a) consanguinity

in the direct line (grandparents, parents, children) always renders marriage between them null; (b) consanguinity in the collateral line renders marriage invalid up to the fourth degree inclusive (first cousins); (c) consanguinity in the third degree of the collateral line (aunts or uncles and nephews or nieces) and also in the fourth degree (first cousins) can be dispensed by the ordinary; (d) consanguinity produces one impediment only, not a multiple impediment as was the case under the former Code; (e) in case of doubt concerning consanguinity in the direct line of any degree, or in the collateral line of the second degree (brother and sister), marriage is *never* permitted.

Affinity

C 1092

Affinity in the direct line in any degree whatsoever invalidates matrimony.

Affinity is that family relationship which originates from marriage; it is the relationship existing between in-laws. The impediment of affinity is regulated as follows: (1) It exists only in the direct line, (foster-father and daughter, foster-mother and son, etc.); (2) It does not exist in the collateral line as would be the case of a man who wishes to marry the sister of his deceased wife; (3) The impediment can be dispensed by the ordinary.

Public Propriety

C 1093

The impediment of public propriety arises from an invalid marriage after common life has been established or from notorious and public concubinage; it invalidates marriage in the first degree of the direct line between the man and the blood relatives of the woman, and vice-versa.

An invalid marriage, and even a notorious state of concubinage, establishes a certain kind of family relationship, at least among the closest relatives of the two parties. Consequently, this situation gives rise to a certain obstacle to marriage out of a "sense of decency," or *public propriety*, which the ecclesiastical legislator acknowledges and makes into an impediment of *ecclesiastical law*. It is regulated as follows: (1) it arises after cohabitation, (2) it applies only between one of the parties and the parents, or children from another relation, of the other party, and (3) it can be dispensed by the ordinary.

Legal Adoption

C 1094

They cannot validly contract marriage between themselves who are related in the direct line or in the second degree of the collateral line through a legal relationship arising from adoption.

In establishing this impediment, the former Code referred to the civil law of the territory. If the civil law prohibited the marriage of persons related by legal adoption, canon law confirmed the prohibition and made it an impediment for valid canonical marriage. The present Code regulates this impediment quite differently. The impediment arises from *legal adoption* regardless of the existence of the impediment in civil law; therefore, if legal adoption has taken place in accordance with the civil law, an impediment arises for valid canonical marriage. But the canon also specifies that these persons should be related by a legal relationship deriving from adoption *(cognatione legali ex adoptione orta)*. This means that if the civil law does not acknowledge any special legal relationship (e.g., right to inherit) between the adopted son or daughter and the relatives of the adopting father or mother, the impediment does not arise; but if the law does recognize a certain legal relationship, the canonical impediment extends to every degree in the direct line and to the second degree in the collateral line (brother and sister by reason of adoption).

The impediment can be dispensed by the ordinary.

5

MATRIMONIAL CONSENT*

(Code of Canon Law, Book IV, Title VII, Chap. IV, CC 1095–1107)

Consensual Incapacity

C 1095

They are incapable of contracting marriage:

1° who lack the sufficient use of reason;

2° who suffer from grave lack of discretion of judgment concerning essential matrimonial rights and duties which are to be mutually given and accepted;

3° who are not capable of assuming the essential obligation of matrimony due to causes of a psychic nature.

In CC 1055–1057 and in our commentaries, we studied the essential elements and properties of the matrimonial covenant. We saw that C 1057, §2 defines the mutual and irrevocable *consent* that makes up the matrimonial covenant as an *act of the will* by which a man and a woman give and accept one another for the purpose of establishing a marriage. Having defined matrimonial consent, C 1095 now defines *incapacity to consent* by establishing three types of such incapacity. Before commenting on each of the three types, the general concept of incapacity to consent requires further discussion.

*The commentaries to CC 1695–1108 substantially follow Dr. P. J. Viladrich's commentaries in *Código de Derecho Canónico*, EUNSA, Pamplona (Spain) 1983.

1. Incapacity to Consent, in General

The act of a person is said to be human (not merely mechanical or instinctive) when a person possessing sufficient *knowledge* about an object, *freely chooses* this object. But for a person to be the true and sufficient cause of his or her own actions and to be responsible for them, *knowledge* and *free* choice must be proportionate to the object that is known and willed. The law acknowledges the need of this proportionality in several instances. For example, an eight-year-old child is presumed to have the use of reason and is therefore psychologically capable of a number of true human acts for which the child is morally responsible, but the same child is neither morally nor legally responsible for other acts (e.g., contracts) for which knowledge and free will must be *proportionate* to the object that is known and willed.

Since valid matrimonial consent, therefore, must be a free act of the will proportionate to the essence of the matrimonial covenant, *incapacity to consent* exists when a person is so afflicted by some defect or disorder of the rational faculties that he or she cannot elicit a free act of the will *proportionate* to the essence of matrimony. In this canon, incapacity to consent to a valid marriage is defined by the three types listed. The legislator, very wisely, has avoided any psychiatric classification of disorders which may affect valid consent. Apart from the technical difficulties inherent in such classifications, the legislator is interested in defining this incapacity in legal terms, for it is not enough to show that a person is afflicted by some psychological disorder, as defined in psychiatric terms, but to prove that this disorder has *in fact* prevented the person from eliciting an act of sufficient matrimonial consent, the efficient cause of marriage and the key juridic act of the matrimonial contract.

Incapacity to consent should not be confused with a legal impediment. Incapacity to consent is a psychological inability to elicit a morally valid and responsible act; an impediment is a prohibition established by law that makes the act legally invalid. The person affected by an impediment is normally a person who is able to elicit a psychologically valid act.

2. Lack of Sufficient Use of Reason

"Sufficient" here means the degree of development and harmonious maturation of the rational faculties, normally acquired by the seventh year of age, which makes a person capable of a human act and therefore responsible. Not only are infants affected by this deficiency, but also those adults who are afflicted by a disorder that affects the use of their rational faculties and prevents them from eliciting a human act. This may be caused by a psychological disorder or by other transitory or more permanent conditions such as toxic or hypnotic states, drunkenness, somnambulism, drug-addiction, alcoholism. What needs to be proved in all these cases is the lack of sufficient reason at the moment of giving consent, for this is what truly invalidates the marriage covenant, not just the fact that the disorder exists or has existed at some time.

3. Grave Defect of Discretionary Judgment

The object of the marriage contract requires a maturity of judgment superior to the mere use of reason and even to that of the kind required for many ordinary decisions and responsibilities in life, e.g., to learn a trade, to hold a job, to buy a car, to keep out of trouble. This is not to say that matrimony requires an *extraordinary* degree of human maturity, for matrimony belongs to the realm of the natural law and can be understood, willed and responsibly embraced by most people, even if a *perfect* perception of all that is involved in marriage can never be reached. The canon speaks of *grave* defect, not just an imperfect appreciation of the marriage covenant.

The *grave defect* contemplated here is a defect in discretion of judgment concerning the "essential matrimonial rights and obligations to be given and accepted." This discretionary judgment is presumed to exist from puberty, at age fourteen for the woman and age sixteen for the man (cf. C 1096). If it does not exist, there is a defect that renders matrimony invalid, regardless of its cause. The defect must be *grave*, as already stated, and it must refer to the *essence* of the matrimonial covenant which consists of that giving and accepting of one another in order to establish a community of life and love and a legal bond that is one, exclusive, and unbreakable, for the purpose of mutual help and the procreation and education of offspring (cf. CC 1055–1056).

The grave defect of discretionary judgment must have existed at the moment of giving consent. If a marriage is to be declared invalid, what must be proved is not so much the gravity of the abnormality as it affects other areas of life, but the gravity of the defect of judgment as it refers to the essential obligations of marriage.

4. Inability to Assume the Essential Obligations of Marriage

A person who lacks the use of reason or discretionary judgment concerning marriage is not capable of assuming the responsibilities of the marriage covenant. However a person can have the use of reason and may show sufficient discretion and yet be afflicted with a psychological disorder which prevents him or her from making a firm and responsible commitment to the essential obligation of marriage.

This incapacity consists of the following: (a) a true *inability to commit* oneself to the essentials of marriage. Some psychosexual disorders and other disorders of personality can be the psychic cause of this defect, which is here described in legal terms. This particular type of incapacity consists of a real *inability to render what is due by the contract*. This could be compared to the incapacity of a farmer to enter a binding contract to deliver the crops which he cannot possibly reap; (b) this inability to commit oneself must refer to the *essential obligations of marriage:* the conjugal act, the community of life and love, the rendering of mutual help, the procreation and education of offspring; (c) the inability must be tantamount to a psychological abnormality. The mere *difficulty* of assuming these obligations, which could be overcome by normal effort, obviously does not constitute incapacity. The canon contemplates a true psychological disorder which incapacitates a person from giving what is due (cf. John Paul II, Address to R. Rota, Feb. 5, 1987). However, if the marriage is to be declared invalid under this incapacity, it must be proved not only that the person is afflicted by a psychological defect, but that the defect *did in fact* deprive the person, at the moment of giving consent, of the ability to assume the essential duties of marriage and consequently of the possibility of being bound by these duties.

Ignorance

C 1096

§1. For matrimonial consent to be valid it is necessary that the contracting parties at least not be ignorant that marriage is a permanent consortium between a man and a woman which is ordered toward the procreation of offspring by means of some sexual cooperation.

§2. Such ignorance is not presumed after puberty.

Consent is an act of the will, but since "nothing can be willed if it is not previously known," the act of the will requires a previous minimal knowledge of the object of consent. The canon we are now studying determines the minimal degree of knowledge about marriage that is needed for valid consent. If this *minimal* knowledge is lacking, there cannot be consent, for the intellective element that precedes the act of the will is missing.

The canon uses a traditional expression, *saltem non ignorent* or "at least not be ignorant," indicating that this should be minimal knowledge. This knowledge need not be an articulated, educated, much less a technical, knowledge about matrimony, but a knowledge of the following elements: (1) that marriage is a *partnership* or community of life to achieve certain common goals, (2) that this partnership is *permanent* and not merely a casual or transient relationship, although the knowledge that it is indissoluble is not strictly necessary, (3) that it is between *a man and a woman,* that is to say, that this special community of life can exist only between persons of the opposite sex, (4) that it is ordered to the *procreation of children* or, as commonly said, to raising a family, and (5) that this is achieved through some sort of sexual cooperation. This last clause has been added to the words of the new canon which, in everything else, is a transliteration of the old one. It resolves whatever doubts may have existed about minimal sexual knowledge. What the words of the canon mean is that explicit knowledge of the sexual union is, certainly, not required, but only knowledge of a certain union of the sexual organs.

The canon ends with the presumption that, unless proven otherwise in each particular case, the minimal knowledge required for consent is presumed to exist after puberty, and puberty is presumed to be completed at fourteen years of age for the woman and sixteen years of age for the man (cf. C 1083).

Error About the Person

C 1097

§1. Error concerning the person renders marriage invalid.

§2. Error concerning a quality of a person, even if such error is the cause of the contract, does not invalidate matrimony unless this quality was directly and principally intended.

This and the following canons deal with *error,* which is a defect of knowledge, in so far as this defect may or may not invalidate consent. Error consists of a *false judgment* or mistaken estimation of an object. Specifically, the canon deals with *factual error* concerning the *person* or the *qualities* of the person one intends to marry.

(1) There is error about the *person* when one of the parties wishing to marry a specific, definite person, mistakenly marries another person. This situation may occur very rarely but is mentioned by the canon to emphasize that the object of the matrimonial covenant is the *person* and that the matrimonial bond originating from the contract is a bond among *persons.* Consequently, an error about personal identity makes

matrimonial consent impossible and marriage non-existent. With this principle, it is now easier to study the other kinds of error that are more common.

(2) There is error about *quality* when the false judgment or mistaken estimation is not about the *identity* of the person one intends to marry but about one or several *qualities* that the person may possess. This error does not invalidate consent for, as said above, one marries the *person* not the *qualities* of the person. And this remains true even if the alleged quality was the cause of marrying. Now, as we can see, this is a very common situation, since one chooses a person as spouse *because* of some qualities of this person, but one's mistake about these qualities does not mean that in one's mind one chooses another person.

The principle stated above must be understood with the following qualifications: (a) if the alleged quality consists of an *identifying* quality, we have a case of *false identity*, which invalidates marriage. This can happen only when the person one wishes to marry is known only by that identifying quality. For instance, Mary wishes to marry Mr. Smith's son, named John; if John is in actual fact Mr. Smith's nephew there is an error of identity; (b) if the quality is the *direct and principle* aim intended in that marriage, the quality becomes part of the object of consent. For instance, John had no intention to marry Ann until he learned that she had conceived his child. Responding to a personal sense of responsibility, he marries Ann. Later, he discovers that the child could not possibly be his. Since John married Ann with the direct and principle aim of marrying the mother of his child, which later was found not to be the case, his consent to marriage lacks validity.

Apart from these two cases of error, a false appreciation of the quality does not invalidate consent, because the error of the mind does not affect the object of consent, which is the person as stated above. The reasoning that "if I had known the truth I would not have married" does not necessarily mean that "I did not consent to marry," for in marrying a certain person, there is normally more than the appreciation of one or several qualities.

The error treated in this canon should be differentiated from error by deceit, which is studied in the following canon, and error connected with conditional consent, which will be studied in C 1102.

Deceit

C 1098

A person contracts invalidly who enters marriage deceived by fraud, per-

petrated to obtain consent, concerning some quality of the other party which
of its very nature can seriously disturb the partnership of conjugal life.

This is the first time that the Code introduces *deceit* as a cause of nullity
of marriage. Deceit implies error but it consists of more than just a false
judgment, for deceit or fraud, as defined in this canon, implies a manipulation of another person's rational faculties from which true consent must
derive. Deceit or fraud is also incompatible with that community of life
and love to which one wants to be bound by giving matrimonial consent. Not every kind of deceit, however, invalidates consent but only that
deceit that meets the following conditions:

(1) The person intending marriage has to be led into *error* about a
quality of the other party. If in spite of the attempt to deceive, the innocent party is not deceived about the quality, there is no error and no
defect of consent; (2) the error about the quality should have been directly
caused by *deliberate* deceit of the other party or by a third person: if
there is no intention to deceive even if there may still be error, there is
not that kind of malicious deceit or fraud *(dolo)* contemplated by this
canon. Intention to deceive, however, need not be a positive act: an omission can also be intentionally deceiving; (3) deceit should have been perpetrated *to obtain consent;* a manipulation of the will for an act other
than giving consent would not affect the act of the consent, which then
would remain valid; (4) the quality about which there is error must be
one that *gravely* disturbs the *partnership of life* with its essential properties and ends, for these are of the substance of the partnership of life intended (cf. CC 1055 and 1056).

Error About the Essential Properties of Marriage

C 1099

Error concerning the unity, indissolubility or sacramental dignity of matrimony does not vitiate matrimonial consent so long as it does not determine the
will.

(1) As we have seen before, C 1096 contains the minimal knowledge about
the nature of marriage needed for valid consent: the parties must at least
know that matrimony is a permanent partnership of life between a man
and a woman ordered towards procreation by means of sexual cooperation. Error about these essential elements amounts to invalidating ignorance, but a person can hold an erroneous opinion about *indissolubility,*
unity, and *sacramentality* without necessarily excluding any of these in
his or her will: this person can still wish a partnership that is *permanent*

or not casual, that *binds* him or her to the other party in some real way, and that he or she wishes to establish independently of the fact of its sacramentality. This type of error is called *simple error*, an error that, not excluding the will to adhere to the most essential elements of marriage, does not invalidate consent. This is true even when the erroneous opinion may have been the cause of marriage: John, for instance, marries Kathy because, unlike other women he knows, she does not seem to mind if he is not completely faithful to her. This error about an essential property of marriage does not necessarily exclude the will to take her as his true spouse.

(2) But if the error about unity, indissolubility, and sacramentality is one which *positively determines the will* to a marriage deprived of these properties, this error is called *practical error* and it invalidates true matrimonial consent, because the person intends something other than marriage. The error that *determines the will* need not be an error that leads to a positive act of excluding those properties, for this would require a knowledge of these properties, and here we are speaking of error or defect of knowledge. Consider the following case: Amid, a foreign student, marries Kathy, a Catholic woman, without giving a thought to the fact that, by this marriage, he will be forbidden to enter into another marriage already arranged in his country of origin and which he intends to contract following the customs of his country. Amid's consent to marry Kathy is a consent that is vitiated by an error that *determines the will* towards establishing a kind of relationship with Kathy which, lacking unity, is not truly marriage.

This error, or defect of knowledge, that *determines the will* is not to be confused with the "simulation" described in C 1101, §2 which may happen more frequently but is different from the error described in this canon.

Knowledge or Opinion About Nullity

C 1100

The knowledge or opinion of the nullity of a marriage does not necessarily exclude matrimonial consent.

(1) Since matrimonial consent is an act of the will, and the act of the will requires previous knowledge of the object wanted, it would seem at first, that one cannot possibly want an object that knowingly cannot be obtained. In actual fact, however, a person may still want to attain that aspect or parts of the object which are within reach and be able, therefore, to make a deliberate act of the will. If, for instance, John con-

tracts marriage knowing that he is bound by a previous bond *(ligamen)*, he knows that the marriage will be invalid. In spite of this, however, he wishes to enter a permanent partnership of life and adhere to the other obligations of marriage. While the marriage is certainly invalid, there is sufficient consent to make it valid if the impediment were to be removed by the death of the first spouse. Or if Mary marries with the mistaken belief that she is still bound by a previous marriage, when in fact the first spouse had died, she enters that marriage thinking that the marriage is invalid, but she still wishes to adhere to all other obligations. Since there is sufficient consent and, in fact, no impediment, the marriage is valid.

The canon states the fact that knowledge or opinion of nullity does not necessarily exclude matrimonial consent, implying therefore, that in some cases, knowledge or opinion of nullity may, in fact, exclude consent. This would be the case of a person knowing that his intended marriage will be null by reason of an impediment, goes through the motions of the celebration without really giving interior consent, for he has no desires to enter into any permanent commitment. In this case, the knowledge of the nullity has in fact excluded any matrimonial consent.

(2) The principle contained in this canon is specially relevant for the eventual convalidation of marriage (CC 1156–1165) where it is assumed that consent existed and has continued to exist after the impediment has been removed. If in fact consent did not exist, a new act of consent is strictly required by natural law itself (cf. C 1159). It would be incorrect to attempt to extend the interpretation of this canon, as some wish to do, to the so-called internal-forum marriage, or marriage of conscience, with the argument that if matrimonial consent is not excluded by knowledge of the nullity, consent could possibly be valid and constitute, therefore, some sort of "natural," non-sacramental marriage: The words of the canon provide no ground for such interpretation, for the canon does not say that matrimonial consent given by the parties in cases of actual nullity is a *valid* consent; it says only that in those cases "matrimonial consent is not excluded" even if it remains *invalid*, that is to say, not able to produce marriage, for there is more to marriage than the mutual consent of the parties. Christian marriage, by its very nature, is subject to the laws of the Church, and when the Church does not admit the consent of the parties, because of some insufficiency or some obstacle, there is neither marriage nor sacrament (cf. C 1055 and commentary). To speak, therefore, of marriage as something that can escape the divine law and the law of the church and still retain its validity is inconsistent (cf. Sacred Congregation for the Doctrine of the Faith, April 11, 1973).

Internal Consent

C 1101

§1. The internal consent of the mind is presumed to be in agreement with the words or signs employed in celebrating matrimony.

§2. But if either or both parties through a positive act of the will should exclude marriage itself, some essential element or an essential property of marriage, it is invalidly contracted.

The first paragraph of this canon contains a legal presumption; the second paragraph admits the possibility of a "simulation" which, being against the legal presumption, would invalidate the marriage celebrated. However, only a *positive act of the will*, hidden under the simulation, invalidates marriage; this positive act, furthermore, must exclude certain essential *objects* related to marriage. This will now be considered.

(1) *The positive act of the will*. A mere wishful thought, a lack of interest, a diffident attitude towards the objects mentioned in the canon would not constitute a *positive act* of exclusion.

(2) *The things excluded:*

(a) *Marriage itself.* When marriage itself is excluded there is *complete simulation*. It consists of a positive act of the will not to establish a matrimonial bond. This can happen when two persons wish to marry to obtain only certain civil effects derived from marriage. For instance, Rosita, a Mexican woman, marries John, a United States citizen. With the exclusive purpose of obtaining acceptance from their Catholic parents and greater credibility from immigration authorities, she agrees to be married in a Catholic wedding although she has no intention of establishing any matrimonial bond. The marriage celebration would be invalid by reason of "total simulation." It should be added that such simulation is gravely sinful and constitutes a canonical crime to be punished with just penalties (cf. C 1379).

(b) *An essential element* of matrimony, that is to say, the rights and duties concerning the conjugal act, to sharing a common life, or the procreation and education of offspring. These are the rights and duties which, as noted before, are mutual, permanent, exclusive, and irrevocable (cf. C 1056).

(c) *An essential property.* A positive act excluding *unity* would exist if a person were to reserve to oneself the right to have more than one spouse or the right to have sexual relations with other than one's spouse. A positive act of excluding *indissolubility* would exist if a person had the intention to break the matrimonial bond after some period of time (cf. C 1056).

Conditional Consent

C 1102

§1. Marriage based on a condition concerning the future cannot be contracted validly.

§2. Marriage based on a condition concerning the past or the present is valid or invalid, insofar as the subject matter of the condition exists or not.

§3. The condition mentioned in §2 cannot be placed licitly without the written permission of the local ordinary.

(1) "Conditional marriage" is that in which consent to be bound by matrimony is suspended by one or both parties pending the verification of a certain fact or event. The *condition*, or fact or event to be verified, may be *proper* or *non-proper*. (a) It is *proper* when it consists of a future and uncertain fact or event, e.g., "if you finish medical school." (b) It is *non-proper*, (i) if the fact or event is future but certain, e.g., " if the sun rises tomorrow," or (ii) if it is present but uncertain, e.g., "if you are a virgin," "if you are the heir of your parents' fortune."

(2) C 1102 regulates *conditional* marriage as follows:

(a) A *future* condition renders the celebration *invalid*. This was not the case in the former Code, which accepted this condition by reason of the fact that matrimony is indeed a contract and consequently it can admit a future condition that is licit and not contrary to the substance of marriage. The new Code, acknowledging the fact that a future condition brings about complications concerning the *sacramental* nature of this very special contract, has opted to forbid conditions of future and to declare *invalid* the marriage contracted under such condition.

(b) *Past* and *present* conditions can be accepted, but only with written permission of the ordinary. If the permission were not obtained, the person consenting conditionally would act illicitly and in disobedience of the law but this would not invalidate the condition.

In *past* and *present* conditions (e.g., "If you have in fact graduated from college"; "If you are in fact innocent of this crime"), the uncertainty is *subjective* and the fact or event exists or does not exist independently of the knowledge of one or both parties. Consequently, the matrimonial bond is made to depend on the existence of the condition, not on its verification. However, if consent is to depend on the actual existence of a past or present fact, there has to be some subjective doubt on whether the fact exists or not; if there was no doubt but error, we would have a case of consent affected by error as contemplated by C 1092.

(c) For matrimony to be subject to a *past* or *present* condition, it should be established by a *positive act of the will* that has not been revoked. A mere wish would not be sufficient: "I wish I were certain of your innocence," or "I would like you to have a different job." But the positive act of the will making consent conditional need not be explicit nor actual; one need not say, "I marry you on the expressed condition that you are a baptized Catholic," and yet make one's consent dependent on it.

(d) The condition of a *promise* about a person's continuous behavior is considered to be a condition of *past* or *present*, for consent is made dependent on having made or on making the promise: "If you promise not to drink anymore," or "If you promise to resign your job." If the promise is sincere and responsible, the condition is fulfilled and consent is firm, and if later the person breaks the promise, marriage remains valid, for consent was not given depending on a *future* condition, but on the *past* or *present* condition of having made or making a promise sincerely and responsibly.

Force and Grave Fear

C 1103

A marriage is invalid if it is entered into due to force or grave fear inflicted from outside the person, even when inflicted unintentionally, which is of such a type that the person is compelled to choose matrimony in order to be freed from it.

The term "force" *(vis)* used by the canon means *physical* force or physical coercion which consists of violence exercised directly on the body of a person so as to cause an external sign of consent such as forcing a person to move his head or raise his hand signifying approval or affirmation. The bodily sign caused by force would be totally disconnected from any *interior* consent and would be meaningless, and therefore, there would be no true consent and no marriage.

Apart from physical force, a person can be subject to *moral coercion* which consists of *psychological* pressure exercised upon the will by means of threats. Under these threats, the will is affected by *fear* of harm, so that one may consent to an action for the purpose or intention of avoiding harm. The avoidance of harm is the end or determining element of the consent rather than the natural end of the action itself.

If fear is such that it takes away the power of reasoning, the person acts mechanically or impulsively, and consequently there is no true act of the will or consent. But if a person still retains his rational powers, and therefore some degree of self-determination, there is consent although vitiated by fear. In order to protect the necessary freedom of the will required to enter matrimony, the legislator establishes that matrimony contracted with *grave fear* makes matrimony invalid. But for this to occur, the fear must meet the following requirements:

(1) It must be *grave*. The determination of gravity can be considered *objectively* and *subjectively*. (a) *Objective gravity* in turn can be absolute or relative. It is *absolute* when the threat of harm would be experienced by any normal person, e.g., death, mutilation, loss of fortune, loss of reputation. It is *relative* if the threat of harm would be experienced by any person under similar circumstances, e.g., age, health, education, etc. A mature and normally independent twenty-five-year-old woman would not be easily perturbed by her father's threats to cast her out of the house if she does not marry a particular suitor; but the same threat could cause sufficient grave fear to a submissive and dependent fifteen-year-old girl with no relatives or friends.

(b) The determination of gravity can also be considered *subjectively:* given all of the personality and character traits of the individual, and independently of whether or not the fear is objectively grave, certain threats can create a genuine emotional disturbance sufficient to vitiate the free consent of the will.

(2) It must be *initiated from without (ab extrinseco)*, that is to say, by another person, since the purpose of this canon is to protect the exercise of one's free will against manipulations instigated by others. Fear inspired by one's imagination would not constitute an external cause as required by the canon, for example, if one were to consent to marry for fear of being struck by lightning if one were to refuse. Fear inspired by one's conscience would not fulfill this requirement for it would not be inspired from without, as would be the case of one who feels he would be committing a grave sin of injustice, for which he would be severely punished, if he were not to fulfill the promise to marry.

But the fear that is inspired from without need not be instigated by another with the intent to compel the person to marry. The person subject to the threat must intend marriage as *the only escape from the threat*, but the person inflicting the threat need not directly intend to force matrimonial consent. If a man, for instance, gravely fears being killed by the father of the girl he has seduced, should the father come to know about the seduction, and marries the girl to avoid the danger, which is in fact real, there is a case of grave fear inspired from without even when the person who caused the fear had not intended to force the marriage.

(3) It must be the *principal cause of consent* whereby one is coerced to choose marriage to escape from the threat. There must be a relation of cause and effect between grave fear and consent: fear must be the

principal cause, or *antecedent* cause, of consent. If fear is only an additional cause, or *concomitant* cause for consenting to marry, there is no invalidity. In other words, one must have given consent *because* of grave fear, not just *with* grave fear. And since there ought to be a relation of cause and effect between grave fear and consent, if a person received threats but had not feared them and had proceeded to marry, the threats would be totally irrelevant and consent would be free and valid.

(4) The case of "reverential" fear falls under this canon. This is the fear that originates from a relationship of subordination between two persons and from the reverence due to this superior which could be violated if the subordinate were to disobey the superior's wishes. In this kind of relationship, the subordinate may consent to get married for fear of contradicting the will of the superior, in which case matrimonial consent would be vitiated if this fear is both *grave* and the *antecedent* cause of marriage as explained above.

For reverential fear to exist, the following elements are needed: (a) there must be a relation of subordination as is the case between parents and children, guardian and ward, teacher and pupil, etc.; (b) there must be a well-grounded fear of incurring the grave and lasting displeasure of the superior should the subordinate refuse to marry; (c) there must be an actual coercion exercised by the superior by diverse means and actually experienced by the subordinate by reason of his or her inferior position. This coercion need not be exercised for the purpose of obtaining consent as long as it does, in fact, induce such consent.

If the reverential fear exists in fact and, as we said, it is grave and the principle cause of marriage, it invalidates consent in accordance with the prescriptions of this canon.

Manifestation of Consent

C 1104

§1. In order for marriage to be contracted validly, it is necessary that the contracting parties be present together, either in person or by proxy.

§2. Those to be married are to express their matrimonial consent in words; however, if they cannot speak, they are to express it by equivalent signs.

This canon deals with the *external* requirements for the manifestation of consent which are: the presence of the contracting parties in the same place and at the same time, and the use of adequate words or signs.

(1) The *presence of the contracting parties* in the same place and at the same time is required, because in matrimony there are not two separate consents but, properly speaking, *one mutual* consent; hence the

need of a united expression in one place and at the same time. This does not exclude the possibility of expressing consent by proxy, for the proxy represents the person consenting and expresses his or her consent together with the other party to the marriage.

This requirement, however, excludes other expression of consent by means of communication at a distance (telephone, messenger) which do not involve a proxy. Since this canon reiterates the discipline of the former Code in this matter, it is to be understood that this requirement applies to the *validity* of the marriage of baptized non-Catholics and to those who contract marriage with a dispensation from canonical form (cf. Holy Office, June 30, 1949; *Acta Apostolicae Sedis* 41–427).

(2) *Appropriate words or signs.* Consent is *valid* as long as there is unequivocal expression of the will to marry. For *licitness* it is required that consent be expressed with words, other signs being licit only if the parties cannot speak. If needed, an interpreter should be used (cf. C 1106), but the proper words, or signs, should not be omitted.

The legal principle that "silence implies consent" is not to be applied in the celebration of marriage. In these circumstances, silence would imply a lack of consent.

Marriage by Proxy and Marriage Through Interpreter

C 1105

§1. In order for marriage to be entered validly by proxy, it is required that:

1° there be a special mandate to contract marriage with a certain person;

2° the proxy be appointed by the person who gave the mandate and that the proxy fulfill this function in person.

§2. To be valid a mandate must be signed by the person who gave it as well as by the pastor or the local ordinary where the mandate was issued, or by a priest delegated by either of these, or at least by two witnesses, or it must be arranged by means of a document which is authentic according to civil law.

§3. If the person giving the mandate cannot write, this is to be noted in the mandate itself and another witness is to be added who also must sign the document; otherwise, the mandate is invalid.

§4. If the person who gave the mandate revokes it or becomes insane before the proxy has contracted the marriage in that person's name, the marriage is invalid even though either the proxy or the other contracting party was unaware of these developments.

(1) C 1104 requires a united expression of consent between the contracting parties. This united expression exists, as said before, when marriage

is contracted by proxy, for the proxy represents the person consenting and expresses his or her consent together with the other party.

(2) It should be remembered that according to C 1071, §1, n. 7, for a marriage by proxy to be *licit*, permission from the ordinary is required. For this celebration to be *valid*, the following is required:

(a) There should be a *special* mandate to represent the person in the celebration of marriage. A general mandate of personal representation for other business would not be sufficient.

(b) The marriage for which the person issues the mandate must be with a specific person. A general mandate to contract marriage without specification of the person would not be sufficient.

(c) The proxy must have been designated by the mandator.

(d) The proxy must exercise the mandate in person: no delegation of powers or substitution of person is accepted even if the mandate were to allow them (cf. Answer from the Pontifical Commission for the Interpretation of the Code, May 31, 1948, *Acta Apostolica Sedis*, 40–302).

(3) The mandate itself, in order to be legal, must be issued in accordance with either canonical requirements or civil law requirements: The canonical requirements are as follows: (a) it must be signed by the *mandator;* (b) in addition, it must be signed (i) by the pastor of the mandator, (ii) *or* by a priest delegated by either the bishop or the pastor, (iii) *or* by two witnesses.

When the mandator cannot write, this must be mentioned in the mandate and another witness must sign the mandate. This must be done for *validity* of the mandate whether written according to the canonical form or the civil form.

(4) If the mandate is revoked or the mandator becomes insane before the proxy has consented in the mandator's name, the consent of the mandator ceases to exist, and therefore the proxy cannot exercise it validly; subsequent celebration of marriage under these circumstances would render the marriage invalid regardless of the good faith of the proxy or the other party. However, it must be proved that revocation or insanity occurred before the celebration of the marriage; otherwise the validity of the marriage enjoys the favor of the law (cf. C 1060).

C 1106

Marriage can be contracted through an interpreter, however, the pastor is not to assist at such a marriage unless he is convinced of the interpreter's trustworthiness.

The use of an interpreter for the mutual manifestation of consent, or for the benefit of the person who assists at the marriage is permitted if the pastor is certain of the interpreter's truthfulness. No further requirement is demanded by the present Code.

Permanence of Consent in Invalid Marriage

C 1107

Even if a marriage was entered invalidly by reason of an impediment or lack of form, the consent which was furnished is presumed to continue until its revocation has been proved.

(1) This canon establishes a legal presumption of *permanence* of consent when the marriage was invalid by reason of an impediment or by defect of canonical form. Unless it is proved that the original consent had been revoked by a positive act, a marriage contracted under those circumstances can be validated if the impediment is removed and the other prescriptions of CC 1156–1165 are followed.

(2) This presumption may also apply when one enters a marriage with a knowledge or opinion of its nullity since, as we have seen before in C 1100, true consent may have existed, and if that was the case, it may be presumed that it was not revoked. In the case, however, where one has sued the other marriage partner for nullity on grounds of incapacity to consent (cf. C 1095), the petition for nullity is tantamount to revocation of consent, and that marriage cannot, through any turn of events, be validated. For instance: John married Ann in a *civil* ceremony during which John was under the heavy influence of drugs. Later on, Ann entered the Catholic Church and requests a declaration of nullity of the marriage on grounds of incapacity. Before obtaining the declaration of nullity, John who is no longer incapacitated, convinces Ann to withdraw the petition and to validate their marriage before the Church. Even if at this time John is capable of matrimonial consent, it can no longer be assumed that Ann's consent has persevered, and the convalidation contemplated in CC 1156–1165 could not be applied. A new manifestation of consent according to canonical form would be required.

6

CELEBRATION OF MARRIAGE*

(Code of Canon Law, Book IV, Part I, Chap. V, CC 1108–1123)

The Canonical Form

The juridical or "canonical" form of marriage is not to be confused with the form of the sacrament. The latter consists of that part of the sacramental sign by which a man and a woman express their acceptance of one another as husband and wife; the canonical form consists of those legal formalities which, if not fulfilled, render marriage non-existent even when there might have been sufficient "natural" consent. The canonical form is required for all Catholics. This is another example of the right of the Church to regulate the marriage of the faithful over and above the minimal requirements of the natural law. The Church has always claimed this right, and it has made the canonical form necessary for validity since the promulgation of the Decree *Tametsi* of the Council of Trent.

It must be remembered that matrimony is not a private matter, but a social agreement of the greatest importance in the life of any society. The very fact that matrimony is a sacrament, emphasizes its public and social function in the supernatural life of the Church. The present Code, following the decrees of the Second Vatican Council emphasizes the special role of Christian matrimony and the Christian family within the mission of the Church (cf. CC 226; 774, §2; 776; 1063. Vatican II: *Lumen Gentium*, 41; *Gaudium et Spes*, 47–52) thus shedding new light on the power of the Church over matrimony of the baptized by reason of its sacramental nature.

*The commentaries to CC 1108–1109 substantially follow Dr. R. Navarro's commentaries in *Código de Derecho Canónico*, EUNSA, Pamplona (Spain) 1983.

C 1108

§1. Only those marriages are valid which are contracted in the presence of the local ordinary or the pastor or a priest or deacon delegated by either of them, who assist, and in the presence of two witnesses, the exceptions mentioned in cann. 144, 1112, §1, 1116 and 1127, §§2 and 3.

§2. The one assisting at a marriage is understood to be only that person who, present at the ceremony, asks for the contractants' manifestation of consent and receives it in the name of the Church.

This canon defines the *ordinary* form of marriage (the *extraordinary* form to be used in urgent cases is defined in C 1116). The ordinary form consists of (1) a manifestation of consent, (2) the *active* presence of the "assistant at marriage," and (3) the presence of two additional witnesses.

(1) *Manifestation of Consent*

As prescribed in CC 1104 and 1105, consent must be manifested with words or signs which unequivocally express the will to enter into matrimony. This external manifestation of consent is required for *validity*. In addition, the liturgical books provide formulas for the words of consent as well as other rituals that must accompany the celebration: these are required for *licitness* of the celebration (cf. CC 1119 and 1120).

(2) *Active Presence of the "Assistant at Marriage"*

The active presence of the "assistant at marriage" consists of asking for and receiving, in the name of the Church, the manifestation of consent from the contracting parties. This function is not one of jurisdiction, but simply of "witnessing" in the name of the Church the celebration of a sacrament in which the contracting parties are the ministers. He is a "qualified" witness, the "qualification" consisting of the representation which he holds.

This act of representing the Church belongs: (a) to the local ordinary and to the pastor by virtue of their office; (b) to the priest or deacon by delegation from the ordinary or the pastor. Under the term "local ordinary" are included the diocesan bishop, those who head a particular church assimilated by law to a diocese, the vicar general, and the episcopal vicar if his particular mandate includes this function (cf. CC 134 and 368). Under the term "pastor" are included the pastor of a parish or a quasi-parish (CC 515 and 516), the parish administrator (cf. C 540), and the priests who jointly care for a parish under a moderator (cf. C 543).

(3) *Presence of Two Additional Witnesses*

The two witnesses must be present at the moment of the manifestation of consent. All that is required from them is the capacity to witness, that is to say, to have the use of reason and the use of the senses necessary to perceive the manifestation of consent.

Canonical form as described above is required for *validity*, except in the following cases: (a) *common error*, which shall be explained in our commentary to C 1111; (b) extraordinary *delegation to a lay person* to assist at marriage in accordance with C 1112; (c) *extraordinary form* in accordance with C 1116; and (d) *dispensation of form* according to C 1127.

The "Qualified Witness"

C 1109

Unless they have been excommunicated, interdicted or suspended from office or declared such, whether by sentence or decree, within the confines of their territory, the local ordinary and the pastor in virtue of their office, validly assist at the marriage of their subjects as well as of non-subjects provided one of the contractants is of the Latin rite.

Since the local ordinary and the pastor are competent to assist at marriages by reason of their office, their competency is dependent on: (1) the *legitimate possession* of their office, which they lack if they were suspended, excommunicated, or subject to interdict; (2) the *territory* committed to their office: within this territory they are competent to assist at all marriages, even if the contracting parties belong to another diocese or parish and at least one of them belongs to the Latin rite. Outside of their territory, or for the marriage of two Catholics who belong to an Eastern Rite, the Ordinary and the pastor need delegation, like any other priest or deacon, to assist at a marriage *validly*.

C 1110

In virtue of their office and within the limits of their jurisdiction an ordinary and a personal pastor validly assist only at marriages involving at least one of their subjects.

When the office of the ordinary or of the pastor is not an office exercised over a territory but over the persons subject to a *personal* jurisdiction, their competency to assist at marriages extends to all those marriages in which at least one of the parties is under their jurisdiction. Outside the limits of their jurisdiction, they must obtain proper delegation to assist *validly* at a marriage.

Delegation of Faculties to Assist at Marriage

C 1111

§1. As long as they validly hold office, the local ordinary and the pastor can delegate to their priests and deacons the faculty, even a general one, to assist at marriages within the limits of their territory.

§2. To be valid the delegation of the faculty to assist at marriages must be given expressly to specified persons; if it is a question of a special delegation, it is to be granted for a specific marriage; however, if it is a question of a general delegation, it is to be granted in writing.

While CC 1109 and 1110 confer ordinary competency to assist at marriage on the ordinary and the pastor, this canon defines the *delegated* competency that can be given to priests and deacons in the following terms:

(1) Delegation to assist at marriage can be given only by those who are competent by virtue of their office, that is to say, by the local ordinary and the pastor and all those who, as explained above, are included under these names (cf. C 1108 and commentary).

(2) Only those who are legally in possession of their office can validly delegate and only for marriages celebrated within their jurisdiction (cf. CC 1109 and 1110 and commentaries).

(3) Delegation can be given only to priests or deacons who have not been suspended, excommunicated, or interdicted (cf. CC 1331–1335).

(4) Delegation must be given to *specific* priests or deacons. In other words, the person who receives the delegation must be *specifically* identified: It would not be sufficient to say, "all visiting priests," "all priests living at the rectory." The *specific* delegation, however, can be *implicitly* given: e.g., if the pastor asks Fr. Smith to assist at a particular marriage or all marriages under the pastor's jurisdiction, the pastor is implicitly giving him delegation; the delegation in this case is *implicitly* though *specifically* given to Fr. Smith.

(5) Delegation to assist at marriage can be *general* or *special:* (a) There is general delegation when given to a priest or deacon for several or all marriages within the jurisdiction of the grantor. General delegation must be given in *writing;* (b) there is *special* delegation when given for one specific marriage clearly identified (e.g., "the Smith-Doe marriage"; "the wedding at 2:00 p.m. Saturday"). A special delegation can be given orally.

(6) General delegation can be *subdelegated;* special delegation can be subdelegated only with expressed permission of the grantor. No further subdelegation is valid unless authorized by the first grantor, that

is to say, the one who has ordinary competence by virtue of his office. This follows from what is established in C 137, §§3 and 4:

§3. If executive power delegated by another authority having ordinary power was delegated for all cases, it can be subdelegated only for individual cases; if, however, it was delegated for a single act or for determined acts it cannot be subdelegated except by the expressed grant of the one delegating.

§4. No subdelegated power can again be subdelegated, unless this has been expressly granted by the one delegating.

(7) *Cases when the Church supplies competency* (cf. CC 144, 1108, 1111).

Legal competency to assist at marriage, whether ordinary or delegated, is required for the integrity of the form and consequently, for the *validity* of marriage. However, in order to avoid invalid marriages due to error in determining the competency of the assistant at marriage, the legislator explicitly states in C 1108 that the general principle known as *Ecclesia supplet* applies to the faculties to assist at marriage. This general principle is established by C 144 as follows:

§1. In common error, about fact or about law, and also in positive and probable doubt, about law or about fact, the Church supplies executive power of governance both for the external and for the internal forum.

§2. The same norm applies to the faculties mentioned in cann. 883, 996, and 1111, §1.

As can be seen, besides the explicit reference of C 1108 to C 144, the second paragraph of this latter canon refers to the delegation to assist at marriages contained in C 1111. Clearly then, in cases of "common error" and positive and probable doubt concerning faculties to assist at marriage, the *Church supplies* competency:

(a) *Common error* exists when reasonable persons are induced to believe by a certain *public fact,* that the assistant at marriage was legally competent when in fact he was not: (i) For common error to exist there has to be a *public fact,* since otherwise the error would not be common but private. It would seem then, that if there was error about the competency of the assistant but the marriage was celebrated privately, the Church would not supply competency. (ii) There need not be error on the part of the assistant, but only on the part of the contracting parties and others at the celebration. The assistant attempting to represent the Church without due competency would incur a punishable crime (cf. C 1389), but for the sake of the marriage and the general good of those in common error, the Church would supply for the deficiency.

(b) *Positive and probable doubt* about competency. This refers exclusively to the assistant at marriage who, after a careful study of his faculties, may still have good reason to doubt his competency. A merely negative or improbable doubt would be totally irrelevant, for without good reasons against the validity of his faculties there are no grounds for doubt. And if there are good reasons to doubt, but no certainty of his incompetency, the Church supplies competency.

The Church does not supply competency, however, if the error is due to negligence or ignorance, because positive and probable doubt implies diligence to know the law and the facts that determine the competency. Therefore, the assistant at marriage who is doubtful about his faculties out of negligence and ignorance, cannot assist at marriage, and if he were to assist without having first ascertained the status of his faculties, he would incur a punishable crime (cf. C 1389). The marriage, however, may still be valid if it were celebrated with common error, as explained above, for then the Church would supply competency on grounds of common error, although not on grounds of doubt.

C 1112

§1. With the prior favorable opinion of the conference of bishops and after the permission of the Holy See has been obtained, the diocesan bishop can delegate lay persons to assist at marriages where priests or deacons are lacking.

§2. A suitable lay person is to be chosen who is capable of giving instructions to those to be wed and qualified to perform the marriage liturgy correctly.

This canon introduces a new type of assistance at marriage whereby a lay person, and not an ordained minister, is duly empowered to receive matrimonial consent in the name of the Church.

Although there is no precedent in the former Code for this kind of delegation, the Holy See had approved this practice in some particular territories, and for this reason it is now introduced into the new Code with some well-defined restrictions.

(1) The power to give this kind of delegation must be requested by the local bishop from the Holy See. (2) The request must be approved by the Episcopal Conference. (3) It is to be used only for a territory where there are no priests or deacons. (4) If the power is granted, only the diocesan bishop can delegate the faculties to assist at marriage, not any other ordinary (cf. C 134, §3). (5) The delegation ought to be given to a suitably apt lay person. This last requirement affects the *licitness* of the delegation; the other four requirements are necessary for the *validity* of the delegation.

Duties of the Assistant at Marriage

C 1113

Before special delegation is granted, all the legal requirements for establishing freedom to marry are to have been fulfilled.

C 1114

The person who assists at the celebration of marriage acts illicitly unless the freedom of the contracting parties has been established in accord with the norm of law and the permission of the pastor has been obtained, if possible, when one is functioning in virtue of general delegation.

These two canons determine the obligation incumbent upon the assistant at the marriage to ascertain that the contracting parties are free to marry. Specifically:

(1) This obligation falls, first of all, on those who have ordinary competency by virtue of their office to assist at marriages. Before granting a *special* delegation, they must ascertain that the parties are free to marry.

(2) It belongs, in the second place, to the person who has received *general* delegation: together with the delegation, this person receives the responsibility to investigate the freedom to marry of the contracting parties. The grantor of the delegation, however, is not totally exempt from the same responsibility because, he should still be mindful that the delegation of his own competency, which he holds by virtue of his office, should be carried out in accordance with the law. Hence, the person who receives general delegation to assist at marriages must keep the grantor informed each time he is to use the delegation, if possible.

(3) Finally, any assistant at marriage, including the assistant with special delegation, should also make sure that the parties are free to marry and that he is not using his delegation for a sham marriage.

It should be noted that all those requirements are needed for *licitness* of the delegation, not for its validity.

Parish Where Marriage Is to Be Celebrated

C 1115

Marriages are to be celebrated in the parish where either of the contractants has a domicile, quasi-domicile or month-long residence; the marriages of transients are to be celebrated in the parish where they actually reside; marriage can be celebrated elsewhere with the permission of the proper ordinary or pastor.

This canon is concerned with the *place* of marriage, which is not so much the church where the wedding is to be celebrated, for this is treated in

C 1118, but rather the *parish* or community of the faithful under the care of a pastor (C 515).

The parish to which the faithful belong and where they should seek to get married, is determined by *residency* which may be: domicile, quasi-domicile, one-month residency, or simply temporary residency. Since no preference is given to the bride's parish, as was the case in the former Code, the parties are free to choose either one's parish.

With permission of the ordinary, or one of the pastors, the marriage can be celebrated outside the parish of either party. This is required for *licitness* only, as long as the assistant at marriage is competent in the territory in which the marriage is celebrated, as we saw in CC 1109 and 1111.

Extraordinary Form

C 1116

§1. If the presence of or access to a person who is competent to assist at marriage in accord with the norm of law is impossible without serious inconvenience, persons intending to enter a true marriage can validly and licitly contract it before witnesses alone:

1° in danger of death;

2° outside the danger of death, as long as it is prudently foreseen that such circumstances will continue for a month.

§2. In either case and with due regard for the validity of a marriage celebrated before witnesses alone, if another priest or deacon who can be present is readily available, he must be called upon and must be present at the celebration of the marriage, along with the witnesses.

This canon allows the use of the so-called extraordinary form in those special cases in which a marriage is celebrated without the presence of the assistant to receive consent in the name of the Church. However, the other elements of the canonical form should be observed, namely, (1) a manifestation of consent, (2) in the presence of two witnesses. For the extraordinary form to be used the following is required for *validity:*

(1) *The contracting parties must intend a true marriage.* If two baptized Catholics, for example, had no intention of contracting a canonical marriage, but only a civil marriage, in a place and at a time where there is no competent assistant available for canonical marriage, the civil ceremony does not constitute extraordinary canonical form because the contracting parties had no intention to enter into a valid canonical marriage (cf. commentary to C 1127, (2), d).

(2) *A competent assistant at marriage is not available without serious or grave inconvenience.* The grave inconvenience may be on the part of either the assistant or the couple. Grave inconvenience, however, cannot be claimed against an express prohibition, e.g., the prohibition to contract a new marriage before obtaining declaration of nullity or decree of dissolution of a previous bond (cf. C 1085, §2).

(3) One of the two following situations must exist: (a) *danger of death,* which need not be imminent, (b) *inaccessibility of a competent assistant* prudently foreseen to *last for one month.* Even if in fact, the danger of death disappears or the assistant is accessible before the one-month period, the marriage contracted under those conditions, objectively estimated, remains valid.

The second paragraph of this canon prescribes that if a priest, or deacon, is available, he should assist at the marriage. It would seem that by making this obligatory on the parties and on the available priest or deacon ("he must be called upon and must be present"), the law grants him delegation to assist at the marriage in the name of the Church, in which case the extraordinary form is not to be used. This requirement, however is only necessary for *licitness,* not for validity. Furthermore, the priest or deacon to be called and to be present, should be truly *able* to assist at marriage. Ability here means that he has neither physical nor moral obstacles that would impede his assistance: if the priest or deacon were excommunicated, suspended, or interdicted, he would be forbidden by law to assist at the marriage, and therefore not able.

Persons Subject to Canonical Form

C 1117

With due regard for the prescriptions of can. 1127, §2, the form stated above is to be observed whenever at least one of the contractants was baptized in the Catholic Church or was received into it and has not left it by a formal act.

This canon prescribes the necessity of the canonical form whether ordinary or extraordinary, for the *validity* of marriages contracted by Catholics.

Included in this requirement are: (1) those who have been baptized in the Catholic Church; (2) those who, having been validly baptized in a non-Catholic Christian community, have subsequently converted to Catholicism and have been formally received into the Church. Although required for validity, the canonical form of marriage can be dispensed under certain circumstances which will be studied under C 1127, §2, subsequently.

Excluded from the requirement of canonical form are: (1) all non-Catholics, whether baptized or not baptized, (2) those who have defected from the Church by a *formal act*. As we indicated in our commentary to C 1086, non-practicing Catholics, even those whose conduct is notoriously in contradiction with Catholic teaching, need not have defected formally, and lacking this formal act, they are required to observe the canonical form. A *formal act* of defection is to be interpreted strictly as an *external act* by which a person deliberately joins another religion or explicitly rejects the Catholic faith (cf. C 751).

Place and Ritual

C 1118

§1. Marriage between Catholics or between a Catholic and a baptized non-Catholic party is to be celebrated in a parish church; with the permission of the local ordinary or the pastor, it can be celebrated in another church or oratory.

§2. The local ordinary can permit marriage to be celebrated in some other suitable place.

§3. Marriage between a Catholic party and a non-baptized party can be celebrated in a church or in some other suitable place.

This canon and the other two canons that follow, deal with matters of *ritual*. Although "the Code does not ordinarily define the rite to be observed in the celebration of liturgical acts" (C 2), it is however concerned with those matters of ritual that are specially connected with some of the legal effects of the celebration. Thus, C 1118 deals with the proper *place* of celebration of marriage, because of the relationship that should exist between Christian marriage and the parish community (cf. C 1063), and even more specifically because of the responsibility of the pastor who, by virtue of his office, is the one most directly concerned with all the legal requirements of marriage (cf. CC 1108–1111; and 528–530).

According to this canon the *place* for the celebration is determined as follows: (1) For a marriage celebrated between Catholics or between a Catholic and a baptized non-Catholic: (a) the parish church; (b) another church or oratory if the ordinary or the pastor permit it; (c) another convenient place, not a church or oratory, with permission of the ordinary only. (2) For a marriage celebrated between a Catholic and a non-baptized person: a church or any convenient place; no explicit permission need be sought in choosing one or the other.

If a place other than the parish church is used, the prescriptions of C 1115 (cf. also our commentary) should be kept in mind: the assistant at marriage, whether he is the pastor or another with proper delegation, should be mindful that his delegation is valid only within the territory for which he has faculties, and he should avoid anything that would lead to unnecessary complications concerning the validity of the marriage celebrated.

C 1119

Outside of a case of necessity, the rites prescribed in the liturgical books approved by the Church or received through legitimate customs are to be observed in the celebration of marriage.

C 1120

The conference of bishops can draw up its own marriage ritual, to be reviewed by the Holy See; such a ritual, in harmony with the usages of the area and its people adapted to the Christian spirit, must provide that the person assisting at the marriage be present, ask for all manifestation of the contractants' consent and receive it.

These canons are concerned with the effects that the liturgical rites may have on the *validity* of the marriage that is celebrated, the *dignity* that must surround the sacrament, and the pastoral *significance* that must be present in the celebration (cf. C 1063, n. 3). Specifically, the canons require: (1) that the expression of consent of the contracting parties, to be asked for and received by the assistant at marriage, should never be omitted; (2) that the rite drawn up by the Episcopal Conference with approval of the Holy See, should always be observed, except in case of emergency; (3) that the legitimate local practices introduced into the rite be adapted to the Christian spirit.

In the United States, the *Rite for Celebration of Marriage* (Sacred Congregation of Rites, March 19, 1969), as adopted by the United States Episcopal Conference, ought to be observed for *licitness*. For *validity*, the minimum required is that consent be *manifested* according to the established *canonical form* (cf. C 1108 and commentary).

Registration of Marriage

C 1121

§1. After a marriage has been celebrated, the pastor of the place of celebration or the person who takes his place, even if neither has assisted at the marriage, should as soon as possible note the following in the marriage register: the names of the spouses, the person who assisted and the witnesses, the place and date of the marriage celebration; these notations are to be made in accord with the method prescribed by the conference of bishops or the diocesan bishop.

§2. Whenever a marriage is contracted in accord with can. 1116, if a priest or deacon was present at the celebration he is bound to inform the pastor or the local ordinary concerning the marriage entered as soon as possible; otherwise the witnesses jointly with the contractants are bound to do so.

§3. If the marriage has been contracted with a dispensation from canonical form, the local ordinary who granted the dispensation is to see that the dispensation and the celebration are inscribed in the marriage register at the curia and at the parish of the Catholic party whose pastor made the investigation concerning their free state; the Catholic spouse is bound to inform the same ordinary and pastor as soon as possible of the celebration of the marriage, the place of celebration and the public form that was observed.

C 1122

§1. The contracted marriage is also to be noted in the baptismal register in which the baptism of the spouses has been inscribed.

§2. If the marriage was contracted in a parish where a spouse was not baptized, the pastor of the place where it was celebrated is to send a notice of the contracted marriage as soon as possible to the pastor where the baptism was conferred.

C 1123

Whenever a marriage is convalidated in the external forum, is declared null or is legitimately dissolved other than by death, the pastor of the place where it was celebrated must be informed so that a notation may be duly made in the marriage and baptismal registers.

As we have seen before (cf. CC 1108–1111; 528–530), the Code designates the *pastor* as the person directly responsible for the legality and for the pastoral care of the marriage of his own parishioners. Besides other responsibilities, C 1121 imposes upon the pastor the duty to keep the marriage records in good order and to make all the necessary annotations on the matrimonial and baptismal registry.

(1) Apart from other annotations prescribed by the particular law of the territory, the *minimal record* required by general law is as follows: (a) the names of the contracting parties, (b) the names of the assistant and the two witnesses, and (c) the place and the date of the celebration.

(2) When the *extraordinary form* has been used, it is incumbent upon those who ought to be present by law (priest or deacon, if available, two witnesses, contracting parties) to communicate the event of the celebration to the pastor or to the ordinary.

(3) If matrimony was celebrated with *dispensation from canonical form,* the Catholic party who obtained the dispensation is obliged to inform the ordinary *and* the pastor about the date and the place of the

celebration as well as the kind of solemnity that was used. The ordinary, who granted the dispensation, is then responsible for the registration of these facts in the diocesan and in the parish registries.

(4) When matrimony is celebrated *outside the parish* of baptism of either one of the parties, the pastor where the marriage took place ought to send *notification* to the parish where the baptismal records of each party are kept.

(5) When a marriage has been (a) convalidated (CC 1156–1165), (b) *declared null* (CC 1671–1691), (c) *dissolved* by the privilege of the faith (CC 1143–1149) or by dispensation of *ratum et non consummatum* (C 1142), the pastor where the marriage was celebrated should be notified. This should be the responsibility of those officials who have to execute the convalidation and decree of nullity or dissolution.

7

MIXED MARRIAGES

(Code of Canon Law, Book IV, Title VII, Chap. VI,
CC 1124–1129)

Prohibition of Mixed Marriages

C 1124

Without the express permission of the competent authority, marriage is forbidden between two baptized persons, one of whom was baptized in the Catholic Church or received into it after baptism and has not left it by a formal act, and the other of whom is a member of a church or ecclesial community which is not in full communion with the Catholic Church.

(1) This canon forbids the marriage of a Catholic with another baptized person who is not in full communion with the Catholic Church. This kind of marriage, which receives the name of "mixed" marriage, is not to be confused with that contracted between a Catholic and a non-baptized person, which we have studied in C 1086 under the impediment of disparity of cult.

In the former Code, mixed marriages were forbidden by an "impedient," or prohibitive impediment, but since these impediments have now been abolished in the system of the new Code, the prohibition of mixed marriages is treated apart from the other impediments, which in the present discipline are not mere prohibitions but invalidating prohibitions or "diriment impediments," as they are called. The new Code retains the prohibition of mixed marriages because, in line with traditional theological and canonical doctrine, these marriages are an obstacle to the full spiritual union of the spouses (cf. *Motu Proprio, Matrimonia Mixta,*

n. 1). This prohibition, however, is not an *invalidating* prohibition and can be dispensed as we shall see in the next canon.

(2) The distinctive features of a "mixed marriage" are: (a) the two parties must be baptized Christians; (b) one of them should be a Catholic and the other a baptized non-Catholic. According to the words of the canon, the non-Catholic party is one who is "a member of a church or ecclesial community which is not in full communion with the Catholic Church." These terms are to be interpreted as follows:

(i) The non-Catholic party must be a *baptized* person: this should be proved, otherwise the marriage could be invalid by reason of the impediment of disparity of cult (cf. C 1086). Baptism administered in the Eastern Orthodox Churches or in non-Catholic Christian communities is presumed to be valid, but if there is serious doubt of its validity, the matter must be investigated. A serious doubt arises when it is known that in a particular community baptism is administered by sprinkling (cf. C 854), or when in the rite commonly used there is some defect about the matter or the words used, or when the intention of the minister of the baptized adult is doubtful (cf. C 869). It is to be noted that in some Protestant communities, baptism is not conferred until an adult age and a person may have been raised to adhere to some Christian beliefs and practices without having been baptized as a child.

If after diligent investigation there is no positive evidence that the person was validly baptized, we have a case not of "mixed marriage" but of "disparity of cult" which renders the marriage *invalid* if the impediment is not removed.

(ii) If the non-Catholic party had been baptized or received in the Catholic Church and *formally defected* from it, there would arise another complication, because *formal defection* implies an act of apostasy, heresy, or schism as explained in our commentaries to CC 1071, 1086, and 1117. Such formal defections carry the penalty of excommunication by which a person is barred from the sacraments (cf. CC 1364 and 1331). Those baptized Catholics who have fallen away from the faith and have joined an atheistic sect are to be included under this type (cf. Response from the Pontifical Commission for the Interpretation of the Code, July 30, 1934). For the sake of the Catholic party, the ordinary may permit the marriage, but the formal defection of the non-Catholic party must be taken into account for the dispensation to be granted for a just and reasonable cause.

(iii) A person who has been baptized or received into the Catholic Church and has later fallen away from practice, or whose behavior is in conflict with Catholic belief is not to be considered a "non-Catholic" whose marriage would be a mixed marriage. But if the practical, though not formal, defection of this person is notorious, another prohibition arises which must be cleared with the ordinary and handled according to C 1071, §2. In practice, then, the marriage of a Catholic whose defection from the Church is *notorious*, though not formal, should be handled as a mixed marriage. This could probably be the case of those Catholics affiliated to the Communist party who, without being classified as formal defectors (cf. Declaration of the Sacred Congregation of the Holy Office, August 11, 1969) have *notoriously* departed from Catholic belief and practice.

(iv) Finally, the marriage of a non-practicing Catholic who has neither formally nor notoriously defected from the Catholic Church would not fall under the prohibition of mixed marriages and would require no dispensation. This marriage should be treated according to the pastoral practice indicated in our commentaries to CC 1064, 1071, §4, and 1117.

Dispensation from the Prohibition: Declarations and Promises

C 1125

The local ordinary can grant this permission if there is a just and reasonable cause; he is not to grant it unless the following conditions have been fulfilled:

1° the Catholic party declares that he or she is prepared to remove dangers of falling away from the faith and makes a sincere promise to do all in his or her power to have all the children baptized and brought up in the Catholic Church.

2° the other party is to be informed at an appropriate time of these promises which the Catholic party has to make, so that it is clear that the other party is truly aware of the promise and obligation of the Catholic party.

3° both parties are to be instructed on the essential ends and properties of marriage, which are not to be excluded by either party.

(1) *Dispensation* from the prohibition of mixed marriages can be given by: (a) the local ordinary as the canon explicitly states; (b) the pastor, the assistant at marriage and by the confessor in cases of *danger of death* and *when all is ready* in accordance with CC 1079 and 1080. In the old Code, these latter powers were given by CC 1004 and 1045, §3, for all impediments of ecclesiastical law, including the impediment of "mixed religion." With the new arrangement of the present Code of including the canons concerning dispensations under the general title of "diriment impediments in general," and mixed marriage in a separate chapter, a doubt can arise as to whether or not the dispensation of mixed marriages can be granted by the pastor, assistant at marriage and confessor in danger

of death and "when all is ready." Our present canon makes no reference to these emergency cases, but this seems to be merely due to a change in the systematic arrangement of the canons and not to a change in the discipline, for we note that CC 1079 and 1080 speak only of "impediments," with no further qualification, thus including other legal prohibitions or impediments of which the prohibition of mixed marriages is the one that remains; (c) in some dioceses, the local ordinary has delegated to pastors the faculty to dispense from this impediment even when there is no case of emergency.

(2) This dispensation can be granted for a "just and reasonable cause." The change from "just and grave cause" as stated in the former Code should not lead to the interpretation that it can be given for a "slight" cause: the sincere wish to be married in the Church and initiate a Christian marriage is a "just and reasonable cause" mainly when the denial of the dispensation could lead a person to become alienated from the Church. A dispensation granted without just and reasonable cause would be invalid, but the marriage contracted with such an invalid dispensation would be valid, for the prohibition is not an invalidating one.

(3) Before the dispensation can be granted, the *conditions* listed by the canon must be fulfilled: (a) Two things are required of the *Catholic party*, namely, a *declaration* of intention to remove danger of defecting from the Catholic faith, and a *promise* to baptize and raise the children in the Catholic faith. This is a requirement of *divine law* from which no one can dispense, for conscience itself demands the removal of any danger against the faith arising from a common life with another who does not share the faith, and the serious commitment to baptize and educate all the children in the Catholic faith is part of the essence of Catholic marriage. (b) The *non-Catholic party* must be informed of that declaration and promise, so that by being aware of those commitments, the non-Catholic party is bound in conscience to respect the obligations of the Catholic party. (c) *Both parties* must receive proper instruction about the essential ends and properties so that they contract a true marriage.

C 1126

The conference of bishops is to establish the way in which these declarations and promises, which are always required, are to be made, what proof of them there should be in the external forum and how they are to be brought to the attention of the non-Catholic party.

The competence of the Episcopal Conference concerning the requirements of the previous canon is the following: (a) To determine more precisely the terms of the declaration and promise of the Catholic party. (b) To indicate the manner of effectively instructing the non-Catholic party about that declaration and promise. (c) To determine the record to be kept about the fulfillment of these two requirements.

Observance of the Canonical Form and Dispensation

C 1127

§1. The prescriptions of can. 1108 are to be observed concerning the form to be employed in a mixed marriage; if a Catholic party contracts marriage with a non-Catholic of an oriental rite, the canonical form of celebration is to be observed only for licity; for validity, however, the presence of a sacred minister is required along with the observance of the other requirements of law.

§2. If serious difficulties pose an obstacle to the observance of the canonical form, the local ordinary of the Catholic party has the right to dispense from the form in individual cases, but after consulting the ordinary of the place where the marriage is to be celebrated and with due regard, for validity, for some public form of celebration; the conference of bishops is to issue norms by which such a dispensation may be granted in an orderly manner.

§3. Before or after the canonical celebration held in accord with the norm of §1, it is forbidden to have another religious celebration of the same marriage to express or renew matrimonial consent; it is likewise forbidden to have a religious celebration in which a Catholic and a non-Catholic minister, assisting together but following their respective rituals, ask for the consent of the parties.

This canon restates the need of the canonical form for all Catholics and provides for the possible dispensation of this requirement. More specifically, the canon regulates the following matters.

(1) *The canonical form is required for validity.*

This applies also to *mixed marriages* and those contracted with a dispensation from the impediment of *disparity of cult* as explicitly noted in C 1129.

There is an exception to this principle. In the cases of mixed marriages between a Catholic and a person who belongs to an Oriental Church, the canonical form is required for licitness but not for *validity* if: (a) *The marriage is celebrated before a sacred minister.* The reason for this provision is explained by the Decree *Crescens matrimoniorum* (Sacred Congregation for the Oriental Churches, February 22, 1967) "as a means to prevent invalid marriages" mainly, but not exclusively, in those regions where the non-Catholic Eastern Churches are prevalent and where many mixed marriages would be invalid when in fact these Eastern Churches share a common belief in the sacraments with the

Catholic Church. This provision, now incorporated into the new Code, seems to be in line with C 844, §§2 and 3, which, in special circumstances, allows Catholics to receive sacraments from non-Catholic Eastern Churches and members of these Churches to receive the sacraments from the Catholic Church. (b) *Other legal requirements are observed.* It would seem that besides those requirements concerning capacity and consent, which are at the essence of the matrimonial covenant, other requirements concerning the *expression* of consent and the presence of two *witnesses* are also necessary for validity, for these are "natural law" requirements in so far as they constitute the public manner of celebrating marriage (cf. our introductory commentary to the Canonical Form, p. 55).

(2) *Dispensation of canonical form.*

(a) This dispensation is granted by the *ordinary* of the Catholic party. If the place of celebration is not within his jurisdiction, he should consult with the ordinary of the place where the marriage is to take place, who is the best one to judge whether or not such celebration without canonical form may give rise to scandal or to other difficulties.

(b) The dispensation can be granted for *mixed marriages* and for those to be contracted with a dispensation from the impediment of *disparity of cult* as explicitly stated in C 1129.

(c) It must be granted only when the canonical form cannot be observed without *great difficulty,* such as persistent opposition to it by the non-Catholic party or close relatives, ostracism from friends, grave economic harm, grave conflict of conscience, or other similar difficulties. If the dispensation were to be granted with insufficient cause, the marriage would still be valid.

(d) Another *public* manner of celebration should be observed for the *validity* of marriage. As we explained in our introductory commentary to the Canonical Form, every marriage is a social and public agreement which requires a public manner of celebration. It should be noted, however, that this public form need not be a religious ceremony; it can also be the public form of a civil ceremony provided that true consent be given and that the expression of consent and the presence of two witnesses not be omitted. It would seem that the celebration of a mixed marriage with a non-religious ceremony would be a rare event; a marriage, however, contracted with dispensation from "disparity of cult" and dispensation from canonical form may more often be celebrated with a civil ceremony.

(e) The Episcopal Conference is to determine more closely the reasons for granting this dispensation and the minimal elements required for the public form.

(3) *Religious rites in the celebration of mixed marriages.*

(a) The rite to be followed is that prescribed by the liturgical books approved by the Catholic Church. When the canonical form has been dispensed for a mixed marriage or one with disparity of cult, no special rite is prescribed except for the requirement of "some public form" as explained above.

(b) The third paragraph of this canon forbids any duplication and any mixture of religious rites in the celebration of mixed marriages so as not to provoke confusion concerning differences of faith and show consideration for the diversity of beliefs and practices. The "passive" presence of a Catholic priest, however, is not forbidden, and in fact there might be pastoral advantages for his presence, if he is welcome, so that he may explain that the marriage takes place with permission of the Catholic bishop. He should avoid taking any active part in the liturgical rite, using vestments, preaching, reciting any prayer, or giving any blessing.

Pastoral Care of Mixed Marriages

C 1128

Local ordinaries and other pastors of souls are to see to it that the Catholic spouse and the children born of a mixed marriage do not lack spiritual assistance in fulfilling their obligations and are to aid the spouses in fostering the unity of conjugal and family life.

This is a pastoral rule for which we refer to our commentary to CC 1063 and 1064.

C 1129

The prescriptions of cann. 1127 and 1128 are also to be applied to marriages involving the impediment of disparity of cult mentioned in can. 1086, §1.

A commentary on this canon is included within the commentary on C 1127.

8

SECRET CELEBRATION OF MARRIAGE

(Code of Canon Law, Book IV, Title VII, Chap. VII, CC 1130–1133)

Grave and Urgent Reason

C 1130

For a serious and urgent reason the local ordinary can permit a marriage to be celebrated secretly.

(1) As stated previously, marriage is a social and public agreement (cf. introductory remarks to the Canonical Form, p. 55), but this may not prevent the case of a marriage that, for grave reasons, may not be publicized but kept secret and still be a legal and public act known only by a few.

This situation was contemplated by the former Code under the name of "marriage of conscience." The new Code calls it, more accurately, "marriage celebrated in secret."

(2) *Permission* to celebrate marriage secretly can be granted only by the ordinary.

(3) It is granted for a "serious and urgent reason." The old Code required the gravest and most urgent reasons. The example traditionally given would be that of a man and a woman passing as legitimately married who could celebrate their marriage in secret to avoid their irregular situation becoming publicly known. If the grave and urgent harm to be avoided were to arise from a civil law prohibition (e.g., a diplomat prohibited by law to marry a foreign national), such permission should be given by the ordinary only if the "good of souls" is so pressing that it truly overrides the demands of the civil law, for the spirit of Canon law is not to defraud the laws of civil society.

Obligations Concerning Secrecy and Registration of these Marriages

C 1131

The permission to celebrate a marriage secretly also includes:

1° permission that the pre-matrimonial investigation be made secretly;

2° the obligation that secrecy concerning the marriage be observed by the local ordinary, the assistant at marriage, the witnesses and the spouses.

This canon defines more precisely what is to be understood by *marriage celebrated in secret*. It consists of: (1) A marriage *prepared* without any publicity whatsoever. The permission of the ordinary for secret celebration includes permission to dispense from those means of investigation that would alert others to the impending marriage. Specifically, the "banns" would not be issued and no affidavits would be required from anyone other than those mentioned in the canon; (2) A marriage *celebrated* with the attendance of no one other than the spouses, the assistant at the marriage, and the two witnesses; (3) a marriage *known* only by those same persons plus the ordinary himself. The ordinary, however, is not bound to keep the secret in the circumstances described in the canon that follows.

C 1132

The obligation to observe secrecy mentioned in can. 1131, n. 2, ceases on the part of the local ordinary if serious scandal or serious harm to the sanctity of marriage is threatened by observing the secret and this is to be made known to the parties before the celebration of the marriage.

Note that the parties should be notified of the prescriptions of this canon *before the marriage* is celebrated.

C 1133

A marriage celebrated secretly is to be noted only in the special register which is to be kept in the secret archive of the curia.

9

THE EFFECTS OF MARRIAGE

(Code of Canon Law, Book IV, Title VII, Chap. VIII, CC 1134–1140)

The Bond of Marriage

C 1134

From a valid marriage arises a bond between the spouses which by its very nature is perpetual and exclusive; furthermore, in a Christian marriage the spouses are strengthened and, as it were, consecrated for the duties and the dignity of their state by a special sacrament.

By focusing now on the effects of a valid matrimonial contract, this canon reiterates from a more legal point of view some of the doctrinal principles stated in CC 1055–1057. Specifically, the immediate effects that derive from this contract are:

(1) The *matrimonial bond* which by its very nature is perpetual and exclusive. This is true in every marriage, even in a valid, non-Christian marriage (cf. CC 1055–1057, 1141, and commentary).

(2) *The grace of the sacrament.* This is, of course, exclusive to Christian marriage, or marriage between two baptized persons legally celebrated. The spouses are strengthened and consecrated to take up the duties and assume the dignity of their new state. It is precisely in view of the sacrament and its effects that the Church claims the exclusive right to regulate the marriages of Catholics, except for the purely civil effects (cf. C 1059).

Rights and Obligations of the Spouses

C 1135

Each of the spouses has equal obligations and rights to those things which pertain to the partnership of conjugal life.

The spouses are equal partners in those things that belong to the partnership. According to traditional interpretation, this equality of rights and obligations refers mainly to the following:

(1) Equal rights and obligations regarding the conjugal act.

(2) Equal rights and obligations to a life in common or, to use the traditional expression, "cohabitation of bed and board." Except in those cases of legitimate separation, the unilateral separation from common life constitutes desertion (cf. C 1151 and commentary).

(3) Equal rights and obligations with respect to those material goods which are necessary for the community of life among the spouses and for the procreation and education of children. Canon law does not attempt to determine what may constitute this community of goods, for this belongs to the "civil effects" of marriage. The canon simply states the principle that certain common and equal rights and obligations are required to achieve the ends of marriage.

In those matters in which each is called to exercise his or her own specific functions as husband or wife, father or mother, the duties are different and so are their corresponding rights. And among those goods which are not necessary to achieve the ends of marriage, each may have exclusive rights, and the goods need not be held in common.

C 1136

Parents have the most serious duty and the primary right to do all in their power to see to the physical, social, cultural, moral, and religious upbringing of their children.

The spouses have equal rights and duties towards the children. Furthermore, each must make up for the deficiencies of the other. The canon emphasizes the "very grave" obligation and the "primary right" over their education.

The term primary right has been added to the words of the canon, which otherwise reproduces C 1115 of the old Code, to adapt it to recent Church teaching (cf. Vatican II, *Gaudium et Spes,* nn. 50 and 52; *Dignitatis Humanae,* n. 5; *Gravissimum Educationis,* n. 3). The same term appears in C 226, n. 2, which states that "it belongs primarily to the Christian parents to care for the Christian education of their children in accordance with the teaching of the Church."

The rights and obligations of civil and ecclesiastical authorities over education are of natural law in the case of the State, and of divine positive law in the case of the Church, but their function is *subsidiary* to the *primary* right and duty of parents, that is to say, civil and ecclesiastical authorities should provide the aid that parents need without taking away their right and duty. It often happens that in those systems where education operates as a "monopoly," the true freedom of choice of the parents is denied and so is their primary right and obligation (cf. CC 793–806).

Legitimacy of Children

C 1137

Children conceived or born of a valid or putative marriage are legitimate.

"Legitimacy" is defined by the following elements: (1) A valid or putatively valid marriage in accordance with C 1061, §3; (2) Conception or birth within this marriage. The following then, are legitimate: (a) children conceived before the celebration of marriage and born during marriage; (b) those conceived and born after celebration and during the time of conjugal life; (c) those conceived during marriage but born after dissolution of conjugal life (e.g., death).

C 1138

§1. The father is he whom a lawful marriage indicates unless evident arguments prove otherwise.

§2. Children are presumed to be legitimate if they are born at least 180 days after the celebration of the marriage or within 300 days from the date when conjugal life was terminated.

This canon deals with the *proof* to be used when legitimacy is contested or unknown. In these cases, the determination of legitimacy follows these rules: (1) The lawful husband of the mother is *presumed* to be the father of the child born after celebration of marriage and within 300 days after the dissolution of the bond. (2) If legitimacy is contested, the same presumption is restricted to the time periods mentioned by the canon. Consequently: (a) if the child was born within 179 days after the celebration of marriage, the case must be judged without the benefit of presumption; (b) if the child was born at least 180 days after the celebration of marriage, and within 300 days after dissolution of the bond, the child is presumed legitimate unless otherwise proved. It falls on the contestant of legitimacy to provide evident proof to the contrary and lacking contrary evidence, the child is legitimate. (3) If the child was born after 300 days following the dissolution of conjugal life, the child is illegitimate.

The canon does not exclude any kind of proof whether biological or circumstantial as long as it can provide evidence of the fact that conception by the lawful husband did or did not take place, e.g., absence of the husband, impotence, adultery of the wife, concealment of the birth, etc.

C 1139

Illegitimate children are rendered legitimate through the subsequent valid or putative marriage of their parents, or through a rescript of the Holy See.

C 1140

Insofar as canonical effects are concerned, legitimized children are equivalent in everything to legitimate children unless the law expressly states otherwise.

Children that are born illegitimate can be "legitimated" by one of the following legal acts, (1) The subsequent marriage of the parents. A canonically valid marriage or one that is reputed valid, as defined by C 1061, §3, legitimizes *all* illegitimate children, even those conceived or born while the parents were incapable to contract valid marriage. This prescription changes the discipline of the old Code. (2) By rescript of the Holy See. This can be petitioned only when the marriage of the parents is not possible. By any of these two kinds of legitimization, illegitimate children are made equivalent to legitimate children for all legal effects, unless the rescript of the Holy See contains some restrictions. Since the new Code has abrogated the requirements of legitimacy for priestly and episcopal ordination and for elevation to the College of Cardinals, the distinction between legitimate and legitimated children has become less relevant.

10

DISSOLUTION OF MATRIMONIAL BOND

(Code of Canon Law, Book IV, Title VII, Chap. IX, Art. I,
CC 1141–1150)

Under the common heading of "separation of the spouses" the Code of
Canon Law divides Chapter IX of Title VII into two articles: Article
I deals with "dissolution of the bond" and Article II with "separation"
of the spouses *without dissolution* of the matrimonial bond. For the
sake of a more clear distinction, these two different situations are here
studied under two separate chapters. In the present chapter, we include
the two kinds of dissolution: Dissolution of a ratified non-consummated
marriage (CC 1141–1142), and dissolution by the privilege of the faith
(CC 1143–1150).

Dissolution of a Ratified Non-Consummated Marriage

C 1141

   **A ratified and consummated marriage cannot be dissolved by any human
power or for any reason other than death.**

(1) As we explained in our commentary to C 1061, *ratum* refers to
sacramental marriage only, that is to say, to a *ratified* or legally valid
agreement that is at the same time a sacrament. Concerning *consummation* of marriage, the same C 1061 clarifies that a marriage is consummated by a conjugal act that is *humano modo* apt for generation of
offspring, for without this aptitude there is no true rendering of one
another's body to which matrimony is ordained by its very nature.

(2) The canon we are now studying states the doctrinal principle that a marriage that is both sacramental and consummated cannot be dissolved: "What God hath joined together, men must not divide" (Matt 19:6). The same principle is contained in C 1056 where it is stated that indissolubility is made firmer by the sacrament.

An ecclesiastical court can declare a marriage to be *null;* this declaration, however, involves no dissolution of the bond but simply a statement that the matrimonial bond never existed. Furthermore, the declaration of an ecclesiastical court can be mistaken, and a marriage can be declared invalid when in fact it was valid and therefore indissoluble. The error in these cases may remain unknown and marriage nonexistent for the effects of the law, but those who may be certain about the error committed would not be exempt from moral responsibility and from the duty to rectify the error as far as possible.

C 1142

A non-consummated marriage between baptized persons or between a baptized party and non-baptized party can be dissolved by the Roman Pontiff for a just cause, at the request of both parties or of one of the parties, even if the other party is unwilling.

This canon confirms a long-standing practice of the Church. C 1698 of the former Code admitted also a general law of dissolution of the bond by solemn religious profession, but the present Code contemplates only the dissolution granted exclusively by the Roman Pontiff by just cause for individual cases.

The procedure to obtain this dissolution of the bond is initiated with the local bishop and followed eventually by the Sacred Congregation for the Sacraments, which has the responsibility to judge about (1) the non-consummation of marriage and (2) the existence of a just cause. These two requirements are necessary for validity of the dispensation granted by the Roman Pontiff. The justice and gravity of the cause of dissolution must be judged in each particular case with due consideration of all the circumstances and in accordance with the procedures prescribed by CC 1697–1706.

Dissolution of Non-Sacramental Marriages "in favor of the faith"

As we have seen, C 1056 contains the theological-juridical *principle of indissolubility:* indissolubility is an essential property of any valid marriage, even that contracted between non-Christians; in Christian marriage, this property obtains a special firmness by virtue of the sacrament.

While the law of the Gospel confirms and clarifies the natural law, it also imposes on the baptized certain obligations that are of superior rank to those of the natural law, for the purpose of the evangelical law is to lead the believer to the attainment of a supernatural end. By baptism, a person becomes a member of the People of God thus entering into a supernatural community that is ruled by a superior law. In what refers to marriage, the bond acquired by baptism prevails over the natural bond of marriage should any grave conflict arise between the two. This is the theological-juridical principle of the "favor of the faith" which negatively stated means that should a grave conflict arise between the natural bond of marriage and the supernatural bond of baptism, the former can be dissolved "in favor of the faith." Although the application of this principle should always be exceptional, it is based both in Scripture and in the practice of the Church.

The scriptural basis for the "favor of the faith" is found in the so-called pauline privilege of 1 Cor 7:12-16. The practice of the Church is based, according to the common doctrine, on the ministerial power of the Roman Pontiff whose particular function is to interpret the natural law under the light of divine-positive law and to exercise the power "to bind and to loose" with a view to the supernatural end of the Christian vocation.

In the following pages, we shall study the different types of dissolution of non-sacramental marriages in favor of the faith. These are: (1) the dissolution by pauline privilege (CC 1143–1147), (2) the dissolution of polygamous marriages (C 1148), (3) the dissolution of natural marriages by captivity or persecution (C 1149), and (4) other cases of dissolution granted by the Sacred Congregation of the Doctrine of the Faith.

Pauline Privilege

C 1143

§1. A marriage entered by two non-baptized persons is dissolved by means of the pauline privilege in favor of the faith of a party who has received baptism by the very fact that a new marriage is contracted by the party who has been baptized, provided the non-baptized party departs.

§2. The non-baptized party is considered to have departed if he or she does not wish to cohabit with the baptized party or does not wish to cohabit in peace without insult to the Creator unless, after receiving baptism, the baptized party gave the other party a just cause for departure.

Based upon the text of 1 Cor 7:12-16, the Church has traditionally claimed the right to dissolve the natural bond of marriage acquired by two unbaptized persons, when one is subsequently baptized and the "un-believer departs . . . for a brother or sister is not under bondage in such cases" (1 Cor 7:15). This form of dissolution of the matrimonial bond receives the name of Pauline privilege. The following is required for the privilege to apply:

(1) Matrimony should have been contracted by *two unbaptized persons*, one of whom is subsequently baptized: it does not apply when one of the parties was baptized before contracting marriage, nor if the two parties are eventually baptized before separation occurs.

(2) The unbaptized spouse should have *separated* or been unwilling to live peacefully with the baptized party: separation or unwillingness to live peacefully should not originate in the baptized spouse; furthermore, if the baptized party is the unjust cause of separation by the unbaptized spouse, the Pauline privilege cannot be applied. For instance, if Sarah after baptism commits adultery, and this is the cause of the separation by Gabriel, Sarah has no right to seek dissolution of the bond.

The canon speaks about unwillingness on the part of the unbaptized person to "cohabit in peace without insult to the Creator." This means that continuance of cohabitation with the unbaptized spouse carries no danger of perversion of the baptized spouse or of the children. Peaceful cohabitation "without insult to the Creator" would not exist if the baptized party was prevented from practicing the faith, or from educating the children in the faith or was forced into dishonest conjugal practices, criminal actions, or other such offenses.

(3) A *new marriage* by the baptized party. The previous matrimonial bond is not dissolved by the fact that the unbaptized spouse has separated but only by a new marriage on the part of the baptized party. The practical consequences of this are obvious and important: if a new marriage has not taken place, the unbaptized party can return or agree to peaceful cohabitation for the marriage has never been dissolved. This "return," however, does not prevent an eventual dissolution if just cause would arise again, as we shall see under C 1146, §2.

C 1144

§1. In order for the baptized party to contract a new marriage validly, the non-baptized party must always be interrogated on the following points:

1° whether he or she also wishes to receive baptism;

2° whether he or she at least wishes to cohabit in peace with the baptized party without insult to the Creator.

§2. This interrogation must take place after baptism; for a serious reason, however, the local ordinary can permit this interrogation to take place before the baptism, or even dispense from this interrogation either before or after the baptism, provided it is evident in light of at least a summary and extra-judicial process, that it cannot take place or that it would be useless.

This canon requires:

(1) That *interpellations* (or "interrogation") precede the new intended marriage: this interpellation consists of the two questions listed in the first paragraph of the canon which must be asked to the unbaptized spouse.

(2) The interpellations are necessary for the *validity* of the new marriage. If they are omitted without just cause and the baptized party contracts a new marriage by his or her own authority, the second marriage is invalid and the previous bond is not dissolved.

(3) The interpellations can be *dispensed* by the ordinary if it is shown that they cannot be done or that they would be useless for it is evident that the response to the interpellations is negative. However, the ordinary must arrive at this conclusion by a *summary process* which should prove that the unbaptized party is unwilling to be reunited in peaceful cohabitation without offense to the Creator.

C 1145

§1. As a rule, the interrogation is to take place on the authority of the local ordinary of the converted party; if the other spouse asks for a period of time during which to answer, the same ordinary is to grant it while warning the party that after this period has elapsed without any answer, the person's silence will be considered to be a negative answer.

§2. An interrogation carried out privately by the converted party is also valid and is indeed licit if the form prescribed above cannot be observed.

§3. In either case the fact that the interrogation took place and its outcome must legitimately be evident in the external forum.

This canon prescribes the *procedures* to be followed for the interpellations:

(1) *Public procedure:* (a) It is done by authority of the ordinary of the converted party. (b) The unbaptized party must be given a reasonable period of *time* to respond and cautioned that lack of response is to be understood as an unwillingness to be reconciled. (c) Legal proof that the interpellations were made and that the response was negative: this legal proof can consist of testimonies of two witnesses, a letter or other document, or any other proof generally accepted by law. The negative response can be explicit or implicit; an implicit or *tacit* response exists if there is no answer within a reasonable period of time or if the unbaptized person refuses to be interrogated. In this same process, it can be

proved that although the answer to the interpellations may have been affirmative, it was falsely stated and in fact negative.

(2) *Private procedure:* (a) It is done by the baptized party without the authority of the ordinary. The baptized party, however, need not do it personally. (b) This is valid and licit only when appeal to the authority of one's ordinary is not possible. (c) The unbaptized party must be asked the questions of C 1144, §1, and the answer must be negative. What we have said above concerning legal proof and about tacit negative response applies here also.

(3) It must be kept in mind that if these procedures find unreasonable opposition from the unbaptized party, a dispensation from the requirement of interpellations can be requested as explained in C 1144, §2.

C 1146

The baptized party has the right to contract a new marriage with a Catholic party:

1° if the other party answered negatively to the interrogation or if the interrogation has been legitimately omitted;

2° if the non-baptized party, interrogated or not, at first peacefully cohabited without insult to the Creator but afterwards departed without a just cause, with due regard for the prescriptions of cann. 1144 and 1145.

Once the interpellations have been made, or legitimately dispensed, and the response is negative, the Catholic party has a right to contract a new marriage. If the two parties reconcile before the new marriage takes place, the baptized party retains the right to initiate the process of interpellations, with a view to an eventual new marriage, any time the unbaptized party separates or is unwilling to live peacefully.

C 1147

For a serious cause the local ordinary can permit the baptized party who employs the pauline privilege to contract marriage with a non-Catholic party, whether baptized or not, while observing the prescriptions of the canons on mixed marriages.

Since the Pauline privilege is granted in *favor of the faith* of the Catholic party, the new marriage would ordinarily be with another Catholic. This, however, need not always be the case: the party using the privilege retains the right to contract a new marriage even with a non-baptized person as long as the new marriage involves no danger to his or her faith.

The wording of the canon seems to indicate that when the ordinary, for a just cause, grants permission to marry a *non-baptized* person, this permission carries a dispensation from the impediment of disparity of cult (cf. C 1086), and if the permission refers to marrying a *baptized non-Catholic* person, this is in fact a permission to contract a *mixed marriage* (cf. CC 1124–1128). In either case, the guarantees prescribed by C 1125 must be observed.

Polygamous Marriages

C 1148

§1. After he has received baptism in the Catholic Church, a previously non-baptized man who simultaneously has several non-baptized wives can keep one of them as his wife while dismissing the others if it is difficult for him to remain with the first. The same is true for a non-baptized woman who simultaneously has several non-baptized husbands.

§2. In the situations mentioned in §1, marriage is to be contracted according to the legitimate form after the reception of baptism, while observing the prescriptions on mixed marriages if necessary, as well as the other requirements of law.

§3. After considering the moral, social and economic situation of the area and of the persons, the local ordinary is to take care that sufficient provision is made in accord with the norms of justice, Christian charity and natural equity for the needs of the first wife and of the other wives who are dismissed.

(1) This canon incorporates into the body of its text the discipline, contained in the Apostolic Constitutions *Altitudo* of Paul III (January 1, 1537), *Romani Pontificis* of Pius V (August 2, 1571), and *Populis* of Gregory XIII (January 25, 1585). The former Code referred explicitly to these documents in its C 1125 but did not incorporate their provisions into the text.

According to common doctrine, the dissolution of the natural law bond of marriage contemplated in this canon entails an exercise of the special ministerial power of the Roman Pontiff *in favor of the faith* of the party subsequently baptized. The Roman Pontiff exercises this power by means of a general law applicable to all those cases that meet the requirements of the canon.

(2) The dissolution *in favor of the faith* contemplated in this canon applies only when a person was living in *polygamy* or *polyandry* and is subsequently baptized, and when the other spouses are also *unbaptized*. The Constitution *Romani Pontificis* permitted the polygamist to choose any of the wives willing to be baptized and to dismiss the others; the present canon does not require that the choice of wife or husband be restricted to the one willing to receive baptism, and consequently,

we may assume that, if among the several wives or husbands one was a baptized Christian, this need not be the one chosen. However, the canon does not contemplate this possibility, for it twice refers to the several wives or husbands as *unbaptized.*

(3) The new marriage has to be contracted according to canonical form after obtaining the dispensation from the impediment of disparity of cult and promising to avoid dangers against the faith as prescribed by C 1125. All other prescriptions of the law must also be observed.

(4) The natural law obligation to provide for the sustenance of the other spouse is not dispensed.

(5) Although the canon is not explicit, it is to be understood that the previous bond of marriage is dissolved only when the new marriage is contracted.

Captivity or Persecution

C 1149

A non-baptized person who, once having received baptism in the Catholic Church, cannot restore cohabitation with a non-baptized spouse due to captivity or persecution can contract another marriage even if the other party received baptism in the meantime, with due regard for the prescription of can. 1141.

(1) This canon substantially contains the cases contemplated by the Apostolic Constitution *Populis*, which C 1125 of the old Code extended to other cases of forcible separation of husband and wife married before the baptism of either one of them.

(2) It is the common opinion of canonists and theologians that the dissolution of the bond contemplated in this canon goes beyond the range of the Pauline privilege and it consists therefore of a dissolution of the natural bond of marriage granted by the Roman Pontiff by general law.

(3) The privilege is granted in *favor of the faith* and therefore only after one of the spouses is baptized, so that he or she may profit from the benefits of a Christian marriage.

(4) For this dissolution to apply the following is needed: (a) The marriage should have been contracted when the two spouses were unbaptized. (b) Forcible separation should have taken place, making cohabitation impossible. (c) Subsequent baptism of one of the spouses: the baptism of the other party is irrelevant for the purpose of dissolution as the canon explicitly states. (d) A new *valid* marriage, for the first matrimonial bond is not dissolved until the second marriage is contracted. For this new marriage to be valid all other legal requirements (canonical form, dispensation from impediments, etc.) must be fulfilled.

(5) This dissolution of the bond cannot apply if the marriage contracted before baptism becomes *ratum et consummatum*, that is to say, if the parties are baptized and consummate the sacramental marriage before separation.

Legal Presumption "in favor of the faith"

C 1150

In a doubtful matter the privilege of the faith enjoys the favor of the law.

(1) As we have seen in the preceding canons, a natural law marriage can be dissolved in *favor of the faith* by a new Catholic marriage contracted after baptism. This may take place in cases where the pauline privilege applies (CC 1143–1147), in cases of polygamy (C 1148), and in cases of separation by reason of captivity or persecution (C 1149).

For the new marriage to take place, a number of conditions must be fulfilled, but if it is doubtful that these conditions exist, "the privilege of the faith enjoys the favor of the law" and the new Catholic marriage can be celebrated.

(2) For this presumption to become operative, there must be a *practically insoluble doubt* after having made every effort to ascertain the truth. When this doubt exists, the new Catholic marriage prevails over the marriage contracted before baptism.

(3) This presumption, however, does not apply if the doubt is as to whether or not the marriage was a *sacramental* marriage, that is to say, when the doubt is about whether the parties contracting the first marriage were baptized or not. For example: it is doubtful that Nathan has been baptized in a Protestant community before contracting marriage with Sarah, whose baptism in the same community is certain. Later, Nathan is baptized in the Catholic Church and wishes to marry Lucy, a Catholic. If Nathan had been validly baptized the first time, the marriage with Sarah would be *ratum* and "a marriage that is *ratum et consummatum* cannot be dissolved by any human power or by any cause other than death" (C 1141). The presumption to be applied to this doubt should be that of C 1060: "marriage should be upheld until the contrary is proven."

(4) For the privilege of the faith presumption to apply, the doubt must concern any of the conditions required by CC 1143–1149, or the validity of the natural law marriage first contracted.

(a) *Doubt concerning the conditions required by CC 1143–1149.* In the application of the pauline privilege, the insoluble doubt may refer to the actual separation of the unbaptized party or the legitimacy of omitting the "interpellations."

The doubt may also refer to the cases of polygamy among non-baptized persons and, more often, to the actual separation of unbaptized spouses by *captivity* or *persecution.*

(b) *Doubt concerning the validity of the natural law marriage.* If a newly baptized person may contract a new Catholic marriage in favor of the faith when the first natural law marriage was certainly valid, then with even more reason a new marriage may be allowed when the first marriage was *doubtfully* valid. For instance, Nathan and Sarah, both unbaptized, are married by family arrangement. Shortly after, Nathan separates, receives baptism in the Catholic Church, and wishes to marry Lucy, a Catholic. A serious doubt arises as to whether or not there was sufficient consent in Nathan's first marriage to produce a naturally valid marriage. Faced with this *insoluble* doubt, the new Catholic marriage prevails over the first marriage contracted before baptism.

(5) In all these cases of doubt, the presumption is used for the purpose of allowing a new Catholic marriage in favor of the faith. By celebration of the new marriage, the previous bond is dissolved.

Other Cases of Dissolution

(1) The conflict between a natural law marriage and the demands of Christian life may occur in situations other than the ones described in the preceding canons. For this reason, the Holy See accepts petitions for dissolution of other types of cases not contained in the Code. These dissolutions are regulated by the Instruction *Ut notum est* of the Sacred Congregation for the Doctrine of the Faith of December 6, 1973.

(2) For the Congregation to consider these cases and for a dissolution to be *validly* granted, the following conditions must be fulfilled: (a) The marriage to be dissolved must be a non-sacramental marriage. This is the case when at least one of the spouses has never been baptized. (b) If the marriage was between a baptized person and a non-baptized one, and the latter should subsequently receive baptism, the marriage should not have been consummated after baptism, for otherwise the marriage that was originally non-sacramental would have become *ratum et consummatum* and no human power by any cause other than death can dissolve it (cf. C 1141). (c) The "favor of the faith" sought by entering a new marriage must be guaranteed by the usual promises (cf. C 1125) if the new marriage is with a non-Catholic party (whether baptized or unbaptized).

(3) The Sacred Congregation for the Doctrine of the Faith requires other conditions, though not absolutely, for the granting of the dissolution: a case, therefore, can be made regarding the absence of some of these other conditions. The Congregation, obviously, is to judge on whether or not to grant the dissolution should these other conditions be missing. The Instruction, however, warns that special circumstances must exist for the dissolution of a non-sacramental marriage between a Catholic and a non-baptized person that was contracted with a dispensation of disparity of cult. It warns, furthermore, that the dissolution of such marriage will not be granted if the Catholic party seeks to enter a new marriage with another unbaptized person who is not a convert; nor will the dissolution be granted of a non-sacramental marriage contracted or convalidated by means of a favor of the faith dissolution of a previous non-sacramental marriage.

(4) Procedures to obtain these dissolutions are initiated with the local ordinary but are granted only by the Roman Pontiff through the offices of the Sacred Congregation for the Doctrine of the Faith. As in all cases of dissolution "in favor of the faith," the actual dissolution takes effect only when the new marriage is contracted.

11

LEGAL SEPARATION
(Without dissolution of the bond)

(Code of Canon Law, Book IV, Title VII, Chap. IX, Art. II,
CC 1151–1155)

Right and Obligation to Common Conjugal Life

C 1151

Spouses have the duty and the right to preserve conjugal living unless a legitimate cause excuses them.

(1) *Common conjugal life.*

(a) In stating this right and duty deriving from the matrimonial contract, the canon uses the Latin term *convictum coniugale* which may be translated as "common conjugal life" or more simply "life together." This is not to be confused with the "partnership of one's entire life" or *totius vitae consortium* of C 1055. The right and duty "to live together" is only one particular aspect, though a very important one, of the spouses' "entire life's partnership" or matrimonial bond. While the "life together" may not occur in some cases, and for good reasons, the "life's partnership" or bond is still in force. The absence of common life, however, is an anomalous situation which, as we shall see, can be allowed only for a just cause.

(b) By reason of illness, work, or other just causes, a temporary or even permanent de facto separation of the spouses may exist, without suspending, however, the right and duty of the spouses to assist each other in other ways. This *de facto* situation is different from *legal separation* as contemplated in these canons, which consists strictly of a legally declared *suspension of the right and obligation to live together*.

(2) *Lawful cause excusing from common life.*

By marriage, a couple owe to each other mutual fidelity, mutual aid, both spiritual and material, and life in common; the spouses also commit themselves to the spiritual and material welfare of the children. Any behavior, therefore, on the part of either of the spouses which would seriously harm any of those duties, would constitute sufficient grounds for separation. Specifically, the following are lawful causes for legal separation: (a) adultery; (b) serious bodily harm inflicted upon the spouse or the children; (c) serious spiritual harm to the other spouse or the children; (d) desertion. According to the nature of the cause and considering other circumstances, legal separation may be *permanent* or *temporary*.

Adultery

C 1152

§1. Although it is earnestly recommended that a spouse, moved by Christian charity and a concern for the good of the family, not refuse pardon to an adulterous partner and not break up conjugal life, nevertheless, if the spouse has not expressly or tacitly condoned the misdeed of the other spouse, the former does have the right to sever conjugal living, unless he or she consented to the adultery, gave cause for it, or likewise committed adultery.

§2. Tacit condonation exists if the innocent spouse, after having become aware of the adultery, continued voluntarily to live with the other spouse in marital affection. Tacit condonation is presumed if the innocent spouse continued conjugal living for a period of six months and has not had recourse to ecclesiastical or civil authority.

§3. If the innocent spouse spontaneously severed conjugal living, that spouse within six months is to bring a suit for separation before the competent ecclesiastical authority; this authority, after having investigated all the circumstances, is to decide whether the innocent spouse can be induced to forgive the misdeed and not to prolong the separation permanently.

(1) Adultery constitutes an act against the very nature of marriage by which the spouses become "one flesh" and is an injury to the innocent spouse. Consequently, it is sufficient ground for *permanent separation*, which however is not recommended. Furthermore, permanent separation requires the approval of the competent ecclesiastical authority.

(2) Adultery is a cause of legal separation only when it is *formal* and *consummated:* (a) It is *formal* when it is committed knowingly and freely.

Thus a case of mistaken identity or a case of rape would not constitute adultery. (b) It is *consummated* when there is sexual union, but not when there have been only immodest actions or when the sin has been committed only "in intention," i.e., mentally.

(3) The innocent party has a *right* to suspend common conjugal life by his or her own authority. The canon upholds this right, but it does not recommend its use. Rather, it encourages the innocent party to forgive the injury moved by Christian charity and concern for the good of the family.

(4) The *right* to separate in case of adultery is lost: (a) If the offended spouse expressly or tacitly *condones* the offense. This approval *exists* if the offended spouse, after becoming aware of the adultery, willingly engages in a marital relationship with the offending spouse. It is *presumed* to exist if common conjugal life continues for six months without using the right to separate. (b) If the offended spouse consented to the adultery. (c) If the offended spouse had been a proximate and direct cause of the adultery, e.g., by neglect of the guilty spouse. (d) If the offended spouse had also committed adultery.

(5) Although the innocent spouse has the right to separate on his or her own authority, the third paragraph of this canon requires that within six months from the moment of separation, procedures be initiated before the ecclesiastical authority in order to have the separation formalized. This procedure is regulated by CC 1692–1696. The need to use "pastoral means to induce the parties to reconciliation and to resume conjugal life" is reiterated by C 1695. The innocent party should be persuaded, if possible, not to make the separation permanent.

Other Causes for Legal Separation

C 1153

§1. If either of the spouses causes serious danger of spirit or body to the other spouse or to the children, or otherwise renders common life too hard, that spouse gives the other a legitimate cause for separating in virtue of a decree of the local ordinary, or even on his or her own authority if there is danger in delay.

§2. In all cases, when the reason for the separation ceases to exist, conjugal living is to be restored unless ecclesiastical authority decides otherwise.

(1) This canon lists in general terms the causes for *temporal* separation: (a) Danger of grave spiritual harm to the spouse or the children, as would be the case when the offending spouse leads an immoral or criminal life, or deliberately undermines the faith of the children. (b) Danger of serious bodily harm to the spouse or the children; for instance, by physical

violence against any of them, or reckless and dangerous behavior. (c) Great suffering inflicted upon the family by an unjust behavior which makes life very difficult, even if no grave danger of spiritual or corporal harm can be determined. (d) Desertion of the spouse is a manifest offense against the right to a common life, but it cannot be a cause for legal separation because, as the second paragraph of this canon states, the spouses have the obligation to resume common life when the cause of separation ceases. Therefore, since the sincere and peaceful return of the deserter would immediately nullify any legal separation solely founded on desertion, such a formal declaration would have no purpose.

(2) For legal separation to take place, the offending party should be *culpable* of the cause of the separation. In the case of some physical or psychological illnesses, a physical or spiritual danger to the spouse and to the children may in fact exist, and the suspension of common life may be a duty, but this *de facto* separation should not be confused with the legal separation we are now considering. The *de facto* separation mentioned above, requires no formal declaration, and although the right to live together may indeed be suspended, the mutual assistance between the spouses and the sharing of bad and good times could not be suspended, but should be reaffirmed and reinforced. No human judge, ecclesiastical or civil, can dispense from these obligations which, as the traditional words of consent so well express, remain "for better, for worse, for richer, for poorer, in sickness and in health."

(3) Legal separation founded on the causes contained in this canon can be obtained: (a) from the decree of the local ordinary, or (b) on the offended spouse's own authority if there is danger in delay.

(4) When the cause of separation ceases to exist, resumption of common life is obligatory, unless the decree of separation has provided otherwise.

C 1154

After the separation of the spouses, suitable provision is to be made for the adequate support and education of the children.

The canon states a principle of *justice* which is purposely left undetermined, for the practical determination of this duty properly belongs to civil law. The competent ecclesiastical authority, however, should see to it that the spouses are aware of this obligation of justice.

C 1155

The innocent spouse can laudably readmit the other spouse to conjugal life, in which case the former renounces the right to separate.

Even when the cause of separation has not ceased, the innocent party retains the right to resume common life, and is encouraged to do so, as stated several times in the canons already studied. By the exercise of this right, the innocent party renounces the right to legal separation unless a new cause arises.

12

CONVALIDATION OF MARRIAGE

(Code of Canon Law, Book IV, Title VII,
Chap. X, CC 1156–1165)

Convalidation of marriage consists of a legal act by which a marriage that was invalidly contracted is made valid. There are two ways of validating a marriage: *simple convalidation,* by renewal of consent in accordance with CC 1156–1165, and *sanatio in radice,* by an act of the competent ecclesiastical authority as regulated by CC 1161–1165.

Simple Convalidation: Marriage Invalidated by Impediment

C 1156

§1. To convalidate a marriage which is invalid due to a diriment impediment, it is required that the impediment cease or that it be dispensed and that at least the party who is aware of the impediment renew consent.

§2. This renewal of consent is required by ecclesiastical law for the validity of the convalidation even if both parties furnished consent at the beginning and have not revoked it later.

C 1157

The renewal of consent must be a new act of the will concerning a marriage which the person who is renewing consent knows or thinks was null from the beginning.

For *simple convalidation* to take place, the following is required:
(1) That the *impediment* that rendered the marriage null *cease to exist.* A marriage may be null for reasons other than a diriment impediment, such as lack of consent and defect of canonical form, but if it is

null by reason of a diriment impediment, the first condition is that the impediment be removed. This may occur by mere *passage of time* if at the moment of contracting marriage one of the two parties had been under legal age, or by *death* of the first spouse if the impediment was of previous bond, or by *dispensation* if this should be possible according to the law.

(2) That *consent be renewed*. Renewal of consent means that a new act of the will, *wanting* to be married, be *explicitly* expressed. As we shall see in the following canons, in some cases the renewal of consent must be expressed with observance of the canonical form, while in other cases, the canonical form may not be required. Whether it is done in one way or another, *renewal of consent* is necessary for the *validity* of the convalidation in such a way that if renewal does not take place, there is no convalidation and the marriage remains null.

C 1158

§1. If the impediment is a public one, the consent is to be renewed by both parties according to the canonical form, with due regard for the prescription of can. 1127, §3.

§2. If the impediment cannot be proven to exist, it is sufficient that the consent be renewed privately and in secret by the party who is aware of the impediment, provided the other party perseveres in the consent already given, or by both parties when each of them knows about the impediment.

This canon regulates the convalidation of a marriage that is invalid by reason of a diriment impediment in the following way:

(1) If the impediment is *public* (cf. C 1074), the renewal of consent should take a public form, that is to say, the *canonical form* should be observed. Strictly speaking this is not a case of convalidation but of a new marriage celebration. It is possible, however, to celebrate the marriage in *secret* in accordance with CC 1130–1133 if the impediment is public in the legal sense but not publicized or notorious.

(2) If the impediment is *hidden* (cf. C 1074), the renewal of consent is made privately (without canonical form) and in secret so as not to produce scandal. No record is kept of this renewal, because the impediment that cannot be proved does not exist in the eyes of the law. The renewal is to be made: (a) by the two parties if both were aware of the impediment, (b) by one party if the impediment is known by one only. In this last case, however, the other party should have persevered in the consent initially given.

(3) In order to interpret what is understood by "perseverance in the consent already given" by the party who does not renew the consent,

we must recall C 1107 where it is stated that in a marriage that is invalid by reason of an impediment or by defect of consent, *consent is presumed to exist* unless otherwise proved. Only an *explicit* and *positive* revocation of consent stands against this presumption. Therefore, a behavior that is contrary to the marriage commitment does not constitute an explicit and positive act of revocation, as would be the case in severe disagreements, infidelity, diffidence, or the theoretical and ineffective wish not to have married the other spouse (e.g., "I wish I had never married him"). If the act of revocation, however, was one of explicitly rejecting the commitment to live as husband and wife, the convalidation of the other party would be ineffective.

Marriage Invalidated by Defect of Consent

C 1159

§1. A marriage which is invalid due to a defect of consent is convalidated when the party who had not consented now gives consent, provided the consent given by the other party still exists.

§2. If the defect of consent cannot be proven it is sufficient that the party who did not consent gives consent privately and in secret.

§3. If the defect of consent can be proven it is necessary that the consent be given according to the canonical form.

The convalidation of a marriage that is null by "defect of consent" is regulated by this canon in the following manner:

(1) If the defect of consent can be *legally proven*, a new expression of consent must be given in accordance with the *canonical form*. As we explained above, this is not strictly speaking a convalidation, but a new celebration of marriage which, as in the case of the previous canon, can be done in *secret* (cf. CC 1130–1133).

(2) If the defect of consent *cannot be proven*, it is given *secretly* by the party who had not given consent. Secretly means that no one should know about it, not even the other spouse. Consequently, no canonical form is to be used and no record should be kept, for a defect that cannot be proven does not exist in the eyes of the law.

(3) For this convalidation to be effective, the other party should have persisted in his or her initial consent, as we explained in our commentary on the previous canon.

Marriage Invalidated by Defect of Form

C 1160

With due regard for the prescription of can. 1127, §3, marriage which is invalid due to a defect of form must be contracted anew according to canonical form in order to become valid.

This canon regulates the convalidation of a marriage that is null by reason of a "defect of form." The defect of form can be *complete* or *partial*. The first exists when it had been totally omitted as would be the case of two Catholics married before the Justice of Peace; the second exists when having celebrated a wedding in the Catholic Church, some of the essential elements of the canonical form were defective such as sufficient *expression of consent* (cf. C 1104, §2), competency and presence of the *assistant of marriage* (cf. CC 1108–1117), or the presence of the *two witnesses* (cf. CC 1108–1117).

(1) When canonical form was *totally omitted,* the convalidation of marriage should be done by observance of the form, that is to say, by a new celebration of marriage. This, however, can be done without any publicity through dispensation of the banns of marriage (cf. C 1067) and with the attendance only of the assistant at marriage and the two witnesses. If necessary, permission for a *secret* marriage can be granted (cf. CC 1130–1133).

(2) If the celebration of marriage took place, but some of the essential elements of the canonical form were defective, the ordinary way of convalidating the marriage would be through the *sanatio in radice* as regulated by CC 1161–1165 to avoid the defect becoming known to those who were not aware of the invalidity of the celebration.

Sanatio in Radice: Nature of this Convalidation

C 1161

§1. The radical sanation of an invalid marriage is its convalidation without the renewal of consent, granted by competent authority and including a dispensation from an impediment, if there was one, and from the canonical form, if it was not observed, and the retroactivity into the past of canonical effects.

§2. The convalidation occurs at the moment the favor is granted; it is understood to be retroactive, however, to the moment the marriage was celebrated unless something else is expressly stated.

§3. A radical sanation is not to be granted unless it is probable that the parties intend to persevere in conjugal life.

(1) This form of convalidation which, as the Latin expression indicates, consists of a "healing at the very roots" of marriage is done by an act of the competent ecclesiastical authority that makes legally valid a situation of fact that was legally invalid. In the marriage covenant, we must

distinguish between the *will of the parties* consenting to a marriage, and the *will of the legislator* or law regulating the covenant. The consenting will of the parties, which cannot be supplied by any human power but that of the parties themselves (cf. C 1057), is the only cause of the legal bond of marriage. But the law, in its function of regulating this legal relationship, can establish impediments and formal requirements that are necessary for the validity of the contract between the parties. Consequently, a situation of *fact* can exist where the will of the parties would be sufficient to constitute marriage if the other requirements of the law were also present.

The *sanatio in radice* acknowledges the *de facto* existence of matrimonial consent and "heals" the marriage of its *legal* defects, thus granting full legal validity to the situation of *fact*.

(2) The first paragraph of this canon describes the *sanatio in radice* in the following terms: (a) it is *one single act* of convalidation by the competent ecclesiastical authority; (b) which makes renewal of consent unnecessary; (c) contains a *dispensation* from impediment or form; (d) and produces *retroactive effects* to the moment when consent was given. The canons that follow regulate more explicitly these elements of the convalidation.

C 1162

§1. A marriage cannot be radically sanated if consent is lacking in either or both of the parties, whether the consent was lacking from the beginning or was given in the beginning but afterwards revoked.

§2. If, however, consent was indeed lacking in the beginning but afterwards was given, a sanation can be granted from the moment the consent was given.

(1) The very first requirement for convalidation of a marriage that is null is the permanence of consent. Matrimonial consent (the fact that needs to be validated) need not have existed at the start of a conjugal relation, but if given later it should not have been revoked, for otherwise there would be nothing to validate.

(2) *Sanatio in radice*, however, should not be viewed as a way of convalidating a marriage that is invalid by defect of *consent* only. Rather, this convalidation is more often applied to a marriage that was null by reason of either an impediment or defect of form and *in addition* by defect of consent. Consider for instance the following case: Bill, unbaptized, married Ann, a Catholic, because she was pregnant with his child. Intending only a temporary relationship for the purpose of legitimizing the child, they marry without a dispensation from the impediment of disparity of cult. As time passes, he wishes to be permanently married to

Ann. The marriage was invalid by reason of lack of consent, and by the impediment of disparity of cult, but since now consent exists, a *sanatio in radice* would provide dispensation of the impediment and would validate the marriage with no need of renewing consent.

C 1163

§1. A marriage which is invalid due to an impediment or due to defect of legitimate form can be sanated provided the consent of each party continues to exist.

§2. A marriage which is invalid due to an impediment of the natural law or of divine positive law can be sanated only after the impediment has ceased to exist.

(1) The *sanatio in radice* involves a dispensation from the law. Therefore it can be granted only by the ecclesiastical authority that has the power to dispense from canonical form and from impediments of ecclesiastical law, but since ecclesiastical authority cannot dispense from giving proper matrimonial consent nor from impediments of natural or divine law, this convalidation, can be granted only (a) if there is permanence of consent on the part of the parties; (b) if the impediment is of ecclesiastical law or if the impediment of natural or divine-positive law has ceased to exist.

(2) In the former Code, *sanatio* would not be granted to marriages contracted with an impediment of natural or divine-positive law even when the impediment had ceased to exist. In the new Code the healing of these marriages may be granted by the Holy See, but not by the diocesan bishop (cf. C 1165) if the natural or divine-positive law impediment no longer exists, e.g., by death of the first spouse if the second marriage that is being validated was contracted with the impediment of *ligamen*.

C 1164

A sanation can be granted validly even when one or both of the parties are unaware of it, but is not to be granted except for serious reason.

(1) The need for keeping both parties unaware of the *sanatio* granted to their marriage may occur when, for instance, the pastor discovers that some of the marriages contracted in perfectly good faith by the parties were handled with little care for the requirements of the law and were in fact invalid by reason of an impediment which might not have been explained to the parties in the interrogations previous to the marriage, or by any other reason. Having assured himself of the permanence of consent in these invalid marriages, the pastor will do well to ask for a

sanatio in radice without troubling the parties who contracted in good faith.

(2) Apart from these practical applications, this canon shows that the *sanatio in radice*, as an act of government on the part of the ecclesiastical authority, may be exercised independently of the will of the parties who need not be notified of it. If the will of the parties to be married exists as a situation of *fact*, the legal validity granted to it belongs exclusively to the *auctor legis*, the author of the law, or his delegate.

The competent authority of a legal act, however, should not act arbitrarily, and for this reason the canon requires that the *sanatio in radice* in those circumstances should be granted only for a grave cause. To act in these cases without grave reason would be illicit although the *sanatio* would remain valid.

Power to Grant It

C 1165

§1. Radical sanation can be granted by the Apostolic See.

§2. In individual cases radical sanation can be granted by the diocesan bishop, even if several reasons for nullity exist in the same marriage, provided the conditions mentioned in can. 1125 concerning the sanation of a mixed marriage are fulfilled. The diocesan bishop cannot grant radical sanation, however, if there is present an impediment whose dispensation is reserved to the Apostolic See in accord with can. 1078, §2, or if it is a question of an impediment of the natural law or of the divine positive law which has ceased to exist.

This retroactive validation of marriage may be granted:

(1) By the *Holy See* for all marriages in which at least one of the parties is a Catholic. It belongs *exclusively* to the Holy See to grant it, (a) when an *impediment reserved* to the Holy See is involved (cf. C 1078, §2); (b) when the marriage was null because of an *impediment of natural or divine-positive law* which has now ceased to exist.

(2) By the *diocesan bishop* for his own subjects and those who reside in his territory, (a) for marriages that are null by reason of an impediment *not reserved* to the Holy See; (b) for marriages that are null by defect of canonical form (cf. CC 1078 and 1125).

This *sanatio* can be granted even when several grounds of nullity are accumulated. When the *sanatio* validates the marriage between a Catholic and a non-Catholic, whether baptized or not, the requirements of C 1125 must be observed.

The *sanatio* must be granted for each case, not in general for several marriages.

PART II

MATRIMONIAL PROCESSES

Guide to Matrimonial Processes: Canons 1671–1707

Rev. Ignatius Gramunt, J.Lic., J.C.D.

13

GENERAL PRINCIPLES

(Code of Canon Law, Book VII, CC 1400–1500)

The Judicial Power of the Church

(1) The power to govern God's people has been invested by divine positive law upon the Roman Pontiff and the bishops. This power to govern, or *potestas regiminis*, includes legislative, executive, and judicial powers (cf. C 135). There is indeed a distinction of powers in the law of the Church but not a *separation* of these three powers among three distinct authorities, for the Roman Pontiff and the bishops who hold the power of government, gather these three powers together in their own particular office; that is to say, the Roman Pontiff and the bishops are legislators, executives, and judges.

(2) In this present study, we are concerned only with the *judicial power* or that particular aspect of the power to govern consisting of the declaration of the law *(iuris dictio)* over controverted matters. As in other legal systems, the exercise of this power is regulated by certain mandatory procedures which must be observed in the resolution of controversies. The object of these procedures is (a) "to pursue or vindicate rights, or to declare a legal fact; (b) to impose or declare the penalty for offenses" (cf. C 1400). These procedures can take two forms: the judicial procedure and the administrative procedure. The *judicial procedure* is to be followed when two parties submit their legal controversy to the decision of an ecclesiastical court of law; the *administrative procedure* is to be followed when a party requests from the competent ecclesiastical superior a particular ruling declaring a right or granting a grace. The

111

Code of Canon Law regulates the judicial processes in detail as well as some administrative processes concerning *special* cases; other administrative processes follow procedures regulated by particular laws.

(3) The Church claims its own and exclusive right to judge about spiritual matters and those that are linked to the spiritual (cf. C 1401). The power to "declare the law" when a controversy arises upon these matters belongs to the Roman Pontiff and to the local bishop, and to those legally empowered to exercise the judicial function in their name.

(a) *In each diocese,* the bishop holds ordinary judicial power: he is the local ecclesiastical judge who can decide controversies either by himself or by others (cf. C 1419). The bishop, however, must designate a judicial vicar, or *officialis* who, together with an established court of law known as the diocesan tribunal, hears all cases at the first grade of the trial or, as is technically designated, *prima instantia.* With the consent of the Holy See, one tribunal may be established to serve several dioceses (cf. C 1423).

Cases heard *prima instantia* by the diocesan tribunals may be appealed and heard at the second grade of the trial, or *secunda instantia,* by the archdiocesan, or metropolitan, tribunal of their own ecclesiastical province (cf. C 1438, 1), or by the corresponding regional tribunal which the Episcopal Conference may establish with consent from the Holy See (cf. C 1439). The archdiocesan, or metropolitan, tribunal hears *prima instantia* the cases within its own diocese; on appeal, these cases are remitted to the tribunal (diocesan or regional) permanently designated as the *secunda instantia* court (cf. C 1438, 2).

(b) *For the whole Catholic world,* the Roman Pontiff is the supreme judge by reason of his primacy. He judges by himself, through the courts of the Holy See, or through other judges he may designate (cf. C 1442). The courts of the Holy See are: (i) The Roman Rota, which is the ordinary court of the Roman Pontiff to receive appeals to his supreme judicial authority (cf. CC 1443–1444); (ii) The Supreme Tribunal of the Apostolic Signature, which is the last court of appeals in both judicial and administrative processes (cf. C 1445).

Attribution of Competency among Ecclesiastical Courts

(1) It belongs to the ecclesiastical courts to judge matters that are spiritual, but not all ecclesiastical courts are equally competent in all canonical controversies; their competency being determined by the following criteria:

(a) The *matter* under judgment. Some matters are reserved to the Holy See and no other ecclesiastical court may validly judge them. In what refers to marriage cases, the dissolution of a matrimony that is *ratum et non-consummatum* is exclusively reserved to the Holy See (cf. C 1698).

(b) The *person* involved in the controversy. Some persons can be judged only by the Roman Pontiff or by the Roman Rota (cf. C 1405) as in marriage cases of Chiefs of State, which are reserved exclusively to the Roman Pontiff (cf. C 1405, §1, n. 1).

(c) The *hierarchical grade* of the court. The appeal against the sentence of a lower court can be tried only by the lawfully designated court of appeals (cf. CC 1440; 1438; 1443). In addition, if the Roman Pontiff, as supreme judge, assigns to himself the resolution of a canonical controversy, any other ecclesiastical court becomes automatically excluded from the case (cf. C 1405, §1).

(d) The *territory* within the jurisdiction of each court. A diocesan court, a metropolitan court, or a regional appeals court, cannot hear a case which belongs to another territorial jurisdiction (cf. CC 1408–1414).

(e) The *connection*. Cases that are inter-connected are to be heard by one and the same court and in the same process, unless prevented by legal precept (cf. C 1414).

(2) The *matter,* the *person,* and the *grade* of the court determine the competency of a particular court and make all other courts *absolutely* incompetent (cf. C 1406, §2, and C 1440). The *territory* does not always determine the competency of a particular court, for several territorial courts may be competent by reason of other titles (domicile of defendant, place where the contract was closed, etc.); the final determination of competency among particular territorial courts occurs when one of the courts with a competency title is the first in issuing the summons to the defendant. Then the competency of the court is fixed and the other courts are said to be *relatively* incompetent (cf. C 1407).

Concerning the criteria of *connection,* the case is to be heard by the court that is competent over the principal issue by reason of the matter, the person, and the hierarchical grade, or by priority of summons if its competency is territorial.

(3) When disputes over competency arise among courts, the common court of appeals should resolve the controversy; if the courts are not subject to the same court of appeals, the conflict is resolved by the Apostolic Signature (cf. C 1445).

Constitution of the Ecclesiastical Courts

(1) The courts of the Holy See are constituted and ruled by special laws, while the territorial courts are formed and function in accordance with

Book VII of the Code of Canon Law, CC 1400–1752. The organization of the ecclesiastical courts outlined in the following paragraphs refers to territorial courts, but is in many ways valid for the courts of the Holy See which function along many of the same canonical principles.

(2) As said above, the local bishop is the *local ecclesiastical judge* who may judge by himself or through others (cf. C 1419). Normally he judges through the following court officials:

(a) *Judicial Vicar or Officialis.* This person "forms one court with the Bishop" (cf. C 1420, §2); that is to say, he acts in the name of the bishop. As he is the *alter ego* of the bishop in all judicial matters, from the decisions of the judicial vicar there is no recourse to the bishop himself but to a superior court.

Associate judicial vicars, or *vice-officiales*, can also be named. When the *vice-officialis* exercises his judicial function, he also forms one court with the bishop; in other words, the *vice officialis* does not receive his judicial delegation from the *officialis* but from the bishop himself. Therefore, from the decisions of the *vice-officialis* there is no recourse to the bishop but to the superior court.

(b) *Judges.* Depending on the nature of the case, the court should be of *one judge* (cf. C 1424) or a *collegial court* of several judges. In order to constitute these courts, the bishop names *judges.* If the court should be collegial, it is presided by the judicial vicar or by the *vice officialis* to form a court of three or five judges (cf. CC 1425–1426).

It should be noted that in cases that refer to the matrimonial bond, the court must be collegial, except in cases that follow the *documentary process* (cf. C 1686), or when the Episcopal Conference, by reason of the impossibility to gather a collegial court, allows that these cases be judged by one magistrate only (cf. CC 145, §4 and 1424).

(c) *Auditors and Relators.* With the approval of the bishop, the judge or the president of a collegial court may designate an "auditor" whose function is to gather the evidence, in accordance with the mandate received from the court, and to submit the evidence to the court. It is not the function of the auditor to admit or reject the case, nor to formulate it, or in any way resolve it: his function is only to "instruct," or prepare, the evidence of the case for the court (cf. C 1428).

The presiding judge of the collegial court should designate one of the judges of the court to be the "relator," whose function is to report at the meeting of the court and write the decision (cf. C 1429).

(3) In order that the process may in truth pursue justice and avoid arbitrariness, three more public officials should intervene in the process; they exercise their offices without interference from the judicial officers mentioned above. They are:

(a) *Promoter of Justice.* This person is appointed in a stable manner by the bishop in each diocese to safeguard the public good (cf. CC 1430, 1435, and 1436). The promoter of justice, intervenes in the process, when required by law, as a party in the dispute, not as a judicial officer (cf. CC 1431, 1433, and 1434).

(b) *Defender of the Bond.* For cases of nullity of marriage, nullity of holy orders and dissolution of the bond of marriage (cf. CC 1141–1150), a defender of the bond must be appointed in each diocese to argue against nullity or dissolution (cf. C 1432).

(c) *Notary.* This non-judicial court official draws up all court proceedings, citations and notifications, and certifies for their accuracy. The notary is an *official witness* of all documents and records which make up the process; consequently, all records certified by the notary constitute public proof (cf. CC 1437 and 483–485).

Right to Plead and Right to Respond

(1) "Anyone, whether baptized or not, can act in a trial" (cf. C 1476). In the discipline of the previous Code, the right to plead before an ecclesiastical court was restricted to Catholics only; the change introduced by the new Code is specially relevant to matrimonial cases for which a non-Catholic spouse no longer requires permission to act as a plaintiff. The principle stated in C 1476 is completed by two other procedural principles: "Every right whatsoever is safeguarded not only by an action but also by an exception unless something to the contrary is expressly stated" (cf. C 1491); and "a judge may not judge any case unless he is lawfully petitioned" (cf. C 1501), or as the canonical axiom expresses it, *nemo iudex sine actore.*

The canonical process is set in motion by the coordinated application of these three principles: any person, baptized or unbaptized is potentially able to plead in an ecclesiastical court, but in order to plead in fact, one must have a right to pursue or vindicate or a fact to be declared; the lawful claim made before the court is called "actio," and the person exercising this right is called "actor" or plaintiff.

When the judge acknowledges the exercise of an action, another party enters into the process as respondent or *pars conventa.* This party in the process has the duty to respond to the summons of the judge and the right to oppose the action of the plaintiff; this right is called an "exception." In the course of the process, both the plaintiff and the respondent may have other actions and exceptions, which they may present to the court.

(2) The right to plead in court as plaintiff or respondent extends also to minors and to insane persons. These persons, however, must act

through parents, guardians, or "curators" appointed by the court (cf. CC 1478–1479).

(3) The parties may also freely designate an "advocate" and a "procurator" (cf. C 1481). The advocate is the legal expert who can present the case in a legal manner and argue for the rights of his client; the procurator is the representative of the party to enter petitions and appeals, receive notifications and handle all necessary documentation for the party represented. The jobs of advocate and procurator can be held by the same person. C 1490 establishes that ecclesiastical courts should supply a roster of "patrons" whose stipends are paid by the court so that the parties may freely designate their "patrons" from among the names of this roster.

(4) The canonical process is set in motion, as said above, by the action of the plaintiff or the promoter of justice when the public interest is to be defended. It can never be initiated by the independent action of the court (cf. CC 1430–1431). In some processes, the defender of the bond should be called to intervene after the petition is accepted by the judge; specifically, the presence of the defender of the bond is required in cases of nullity or dissolution of marriage, and cases of nullity of holy orders. When the promoter of justice and the defender of the bond intervene, they have all the procedural rights that correspond to the parties (cf. CC 1432–1434).

Discipline to be Observed in Ecclesiastical Courts

Since ecclesiastical courts are dedicated to the pursuit of justice, all persons involved in them must excel in Christian spirit, integrity, learning, and in keen sense of justice. The bishop and the judicial vicar should see to it that these qualities prevail among the members of the court, but it is also the responsibility of the judge who conducts each case to oversee that the same spirit and the proper discipline be observed throughout the process.

(1) In the first place, the judge "is not to neglect to encourage and assist the parties to collaborate in working out an equitable solution to the controversy" (cf. C 1446, §2). The very nature of the office of judge is to administer justice, but justice, which embraces both the common good and the individual good of the parties, is more often served by conciliation than litigation. Consequently, C 1446, §1, admonishes the faithful, and the bishop in particular, to avoid controversies, and places on the judge the responsibility to seek conciliation. A similar admonition is contained in C 1676 concerning marriage cases in which reconciliation is to be sought if at all possible. However, when the public interest

is involved, as in matrimonial or in penal cases, the parties do not have the free disposition of the controverted matter; consequently, compromise and arbitration are not possible and the canonical process must be resolved in a court of law. But even then, the laws that rule this process seek, above all, the good of souls, and the "adversary" form of the proceedings should not be carried beyond its procedural limits.

(2) The recommendation of the Code to use "pastoral" means is not limited to the resolution of controversies: the entire system of canon law is eminently pastoral. For this reason, there cannot really exist a conflict between "pastoral" practice and "legal" precepts, for both are complementary. Pastoral practice consists of an *art* of guiding the faithful to the knowledge and practice of the principles of Christian life, and since legal precepts are norms of conduct given for the welfare of souls, pastoral efforts should be directed to guiding the faithful to understand and willingly adhere to these precepts. An impersonal declaration of the law without regard for the circumstances of the persons whom the law applies, is indeed unpastoral, and so is the disregard for the legal precept when adherence to it may be more difficult because of particular circumstances. Since the law is a "command of right reason" and a guide to right conduct, it is unpastoral to disregard the precept or to bend it, often through legalistic causistry, to attempt to legitimize a wrong conduct. Since the canonical process consists of the administration of justice to particular cases, the ecclesiastical judge and all those connected with the process must excel in pastoral concern duly enlightened by the principles of law.

(3) Judges and all court officials must take an oath to fulfill their duty properly and faithfully (cf. C 1454); they should act with integrity and above suspicion (cf. C 1456); they should disqualify themselves in cases where they may be involved in a conflict of interests and if they do not withdraw from the case, the parties can lodge an objection (cf. CC 1449–1451); they have to act with diligence in the resolution of each case (cf. C 1453) and be zealous for the public interest and for the requirements of justice, including the duty to observe secrecy in those matters known by the exercise of their office which may endanger the reputation of others (cf. C 1455). Failure to fulfill all these duties can be punished with sanctions by the competent superior (cf. C 1457).

(4) The canonical process can be initiated by a plaintiff only, or by the promoter of justice, but once initiated it progresses towards its conclusion by the combined initiative of the parties and of the judge acting *ex officio*. (a) In matters that are of the exclusive interest of the parties, the judge acts only upon petition of the litigants, but even then he must

examine their petitions diligently, set or extend deadlines, and issue decisions and decrees, as required by law, to move the process towards a just conclusion. (b) When the public interest is involved, as in matrimonial cases, the judge may act *ex officio* to exercise actions and exceptions, to ask for and present proofs, and to supply for the deficiencies of the parties, the promoter of justice, or the defender of the bond (cf. CC 1452–1453).

The *ex officio* initiative of the judge however should not interfere with the rights of others: he can never judge without a plaintiff or beyond what is being petitioned; he cannot decide for or against persons other than the plaintiff and the respondent; he cannot base his decision on facts other than those alleged and proved.

(5) Each case must be heard by observing certain procedures mandated by the law to assure that individual rights are respected and that a just decision is reached. Consequently, all cases are to be tried in the order in which they are entered (cf. C 1459); exceptions concerning the procedure mandated by law and the competency of the court must be proposed before the terms of the trial are established (cf. CC 1459–1464) to avoid confusion of the issue and delays in reaching a decision. As order in the procedures is required for a just trial, so is speed in the resolution of the case: time for deliberation must be harmoniously combined with diligence; as the process must steadily progress towards its conclusion, deadlines must be established and observed (cf. CC 1465–1467).

Canonical Processes in the Code of Canon Law

(1) The Code regulates the canonical processes in Book VII under the heading of *Processes*. Part I of this book contains the general principles concerning the judicial process, or *iudicium*, and Part II contains the canons regulating the two types of judicial process. These are: (a) the "ordinary contentious" process; (b) the "oral" process.

It should be noted, that some principles regulating the judicial process may also apply to the administrative process, for they are principles of procedural justice even though the Code includes them within the judicial process.

(2) Part III of Book VII regulates some special processes, which may follow either the judicial procedures or the administrative procedures. These special processes are: (a) matrimonial processes; (b) the process for declaring the nullity of ordination. General norms concerning compromise and arbitration are included at the end of this part.

(3) Part IV of the same book regulates the penal process, and Part V regulates two administrative processes: (a) the recourse against adminis-

trative decrees; (b) the processes for the removal and for the transfer of pastors.

(4) *Matrimonial cases*, which are the object of our study, are to be resolved as follows: (a) Declaration of nullity of marriage must follow the ordinary contentious process, or a special documentary process when the nature of the case calls for this special summary procedure. (b) Cases of separation of consorts may follow their own administrative process, or either the ordinary or the oral process. (c) The dissolution of a marriage that is *ratum et non consummatum* and the declaration of presumed death of a spouse follow their own administrative processes.

14

THE ORDINARY CONTENTIOUS PROCESS FOR DECLARATION OF MARRIAGE NULLITY

(Code of Canon Law, Book VII, CC 1671–1688, 1501–1655)

As prescribed by C 1691, cases declaring the nullity of marriage are to be heard in accordance with the general procedural principles of Book VII, Part I of the Code, and the procedures of the ordinary contentious process as regulated by Part II, Section I of the same book. In the following pages we will often refer to the canons contained in Part I and Part II, Section I as they apply to the declarations of marriage nullity, and in addition, we will explicitly comment on CC 1671–1691 (Part III, Title I, Chapter I) which directly regulate these special processes.

The Competent Forum

(1) *Marriage cases in general*
At the start of the canons dealing with matrimonial procedures, the following principle is stated:

C 1671

Marriage cases of the baptized belong to the ecclesiastical judge by proper right.

(a) Although included under the heading of cases declaring the nullity of marriage, this canon contains a principle of public ecclesiastical law valid for all matrimonial cases of the baptized. In this principle the Church explicitly claims the competency of the ecclesiastical courts to judge over the marriage of the baptized, a claim explicitly made in C

1401. C 1671, however, does not use the expression "exclusive right" of the Church over these cases, as did C 1960 of the former Code and its corresponding Art. 1 §1 of the Instruction *Provida Mater Ecclesia*, which supplemented the former Code in the regulation of matrimonial procedures. In cases concerning nullity or dissolution of the bond of marriage, the ecclesiastical courts have indeed *exclusive* right, for the marriage bond is one of those spiritual realities included in C 1401, but the phrase "matrimonial cases of the baptized" refers also to cases of separation of the spouses, declaration of presumed death of one spouse, or even cases dealing with the temporalities of marriage ("civil effects"), and concerning all these, ecclesiastical courts have no *exclusive* competency. In fact, canon law acknowledges the right of civil law to regulate the "civil effects" of marriage and yields to civil courts in these cases whenever possible, as we shall see below.

(b) It is also of particular interest that C 1671 uses the term "marriage of the baptized" instead of the traditional expression "between the baptized." The new expression is more accurate because the Church judges about marriage cases in which only one party is baptized. Besides, in the present discipline, as we shall see later, a non-baptized party who contracted a lawful marriage with a baptized person may impugn that marriage before an ecclesiastical court without requiring previous permission of the ecclesiastical authority.

C 1672

Cases involving the merely civil effects of marriage belong to the civil magistrate unless particular law determines that these cases can be tried and decided by the ecclesiastical judge when they arise as incidental and accessory.

The Church does not claim competency over the "merely civil effects" of marriage (e.g., property rights of the spouses). These are effects of the matrimonial contract which do not affect the bond nor the essential elements of the marriage covenant, and which the civil law has the right to regulate and judge, for marriage is a contract with important consequences in civil society.

The competency of the civil courts over these effects of marriage is explicitly acknowledged by this canon. Consequently, the ecclesiastical courts are not to accept cases over these effects unless the particular ecclesiastical law of the territory makes them competent. Even then, the issue concerning the temporalities of the marriage contract must be presented to the ecclesiastical courts as an *incidental* and *accessory* issue, and never as an independent or principle case.

(2) *Marriage cases reserved to the Holy See*

(a) By reason of the *persons* involved, the matrimonial cases of chiefs of state are reserved by law to the Roman Pontiff (cf. C 1405, §1, n. 1). By "chiefs of state" are understood, kings, presidents and other supreme rulers of a sovereign nation while in office.

(b) By reason of the *matter*, the nullity cases started in a diocesan court are to be suspended if there arises the probable doubt of non-consummation of marriage; these cases are continued by administrative procedures and remitted to the Sacred Congregation of the Sacraments (cf. C 1681).

(c) By reason of the *hierarchical grade* of the court, the Roman Pontiff is exclusively competent over any nullity case which he may reserve to his own judgment either on his own initiative or at the request of the parties (cf. C 1417) or, when by designation of the Roman Pontiff or by appeal, the case is assigned to the Roman Rota or the Apostolic Signature (cf. CC 1443–1445).

(3) *Nullity cases in particular*

C 1673

In cases regarding the nullity of marriage which are not reserved to the Apostolic See the following are competent:

1° the tribunal of the place in which the marriage was celebrated;

2° the tribunal of the place in which the respondent has a domicile or quasi-domicile;

3° the tribunal of the place in which the petitioner has a domicile, provided that both parties live in the territory of the same conference of bishops and the judicial vicar of the domicile of the respondent agrees, after hearing the respondent;

4° the tribunal of the place in which de facto most of the proofs are to be collected provided that the judicial vicar of the domicile of the respondent gives consent who, before he does so, is to ask if the respondent has any exceptions.

Apart from the cases reserved to the Holy See, cases of nullity of marriage are assigned, by reason of territory, to the diocesan court which possesses one of the following titles:

(a) The court of the territory *where the marriage* took place; (b) or the territorial court where the respondent *maintains domicile or quasi-domicile* (cf. CC 102–106); (c) or the territorial court where the *plaintiff has domicile*, provided that both parties reside within the territory of the same Episcopal Conference *and* that the judicial vicar of the respondent consents after hearing the respondent; (d) or the court *where the evidence is to be collected*, if the judicial vicar of the respondent consents after hearing the respondent.

The definitive competency of any of these courts is determined by "priority of summons": "the court which first legally summoned the respondent has the right to hear the case" (cf. C 1415).

Right to Impugn Marriage

The canonical process, as explained before, can be initiated only by a plea submitted either by a person whose interest is involved or by the promoter of justice (cf. C 1501). In cases of nullity of marriage, the "person whose interest is involved" and who can be a plaintiff is further determined as follows:

C 1674

The following are capable of challenging a marriage:

1° the *spouses;*

2° the promoter of justice when the nullity has become public, if the marriage cannot be convalidated or this is not expedient.

(1) *One of the spouses.*

A third party (another spouse by civil marriage, the children of another marriage, other relatives, etc.) might be interested in impugning the marriage, but only the spouses can initiate the process. A third party may denounce a marriage as invalid to the promoter of justice but has no legal standing in the starting of the process.

In the present discipline, the former restrictions have been eliminated and the spouse who caused the nullity as well as the non-Catholic spouse may sue for nullity. This is in line with the provision of C 1476, which declares that "any one, whether baptized or not, can act in a trial."

(2) *The promoter of justice.*

Since the role of the promoter of justice is to protect the public interest and matrimony is always a public interest issue, it is the promoter of justice's right and duty to impugn a marriage, (a) when the nullity of the marriage has been divulged, and (b) the marriage cannot be validated or it is not expedient to do so.

His position in the process is analogous to that of a party in the controversy (cf. C 1430).

(3) *The impugning of marriage after the death of one or the two spouses.*

C 1675

§1. A marriage which has not been impugned during the lifetime of both spouses cannot be impugned after the death of either one or both spouses unless

the question of validity is prejudicial to the resolution of another controversy either in the canonical forum or in the civil forum.

§2. However, if a spouse dies while a case is pending, can. 1518 is to be observed.

This canon contemplates two possibilities:

(a) If the marriage has not been impugned during life, the validity of marriage is presumed and no contrary proof can be brought to the judgment of the courts. However, if a decision concerning the validity of marriage is necessary to resolve another legal controversy, the marriage may be impugned. It would seem that in this latter case, and in accordance with C 1674, only the surviving spouse or the promoter of justice would be allowed to be plaintiffs in the issue.

(b) If one or both spouses die during the process, the canon allows the continuation of the process in accordance with the general procedural principle of C 1518, and contrary to former discipline: (i) If the death occurs before the *conclusio in causa* (or closing of the case after the evidence is completed), "the trial is suspended but it can be resumed by the heir of the deceased, or the successor, or a person whose interest is involved." The direct reference to C 1518 with no other qualifications seems to indicate that, in these situations, the impugning of marriage is not restricted to the spouse and the promoter of justice but is extended to an heir, a successor, or to anyone with a lawful interest in the case. (ii) If death occurs after the *conclusio in causa,* the trial must continue and a decision is to be reached.

The Ordinary Contentious Process

C 1676

Before accepting a case and whenever there seems to be hope of a successful outcome, the judge is to use pastoral means to induce the spouses, if at all possible, to convalidate the marriage and to restore conjugal living.

Paradoxically, the first concern of canonical procedural law is to avoid suits and to resolve controversies outside the canonical process (cf. C 1446, §1). In matrimonial cases, however, this cannot be achieved by compromise or arbitration, for matrimony concerns the public interest and the matter in question is not under the free dispositions of the parties; consequently, the controversy can only be resolved, if at all possible, by validation of marriage or by reconciliation (cf. C 1715). To this purpose, the law urges the judge, if there is hope for success, to use all pastoral means before accepting litigation over marriage.

(1) *First Stage*

(a) *The Petition Introducing the Case*

(i) As we have already mentioned, a suit can be initiated only by petition of the interested party or by the promoter of justice to a competent judge (cf. C 1501). This petition, presented in written form and containing the object of the controversy, is called the *libellus* (cf. C 1502). The court, however, may admit an oral petition which is then drawn up and officially certified by the notary, (cf. C 1503). According to C 1504, a *libellus* which introduces a suit must:

> 1. express before which judge the case is being introduced, what is being petitioned and by whom the petition is being made;
> 2. indicate the basis for the petitioner's right and at least in general the facts and proofs which will be used to prove what has been alleged;
> 3. be signed by the petitioner or procurator, adding the day, month, and year, as well as the address of the petitioner or procurator or the place where they say they reside for the purpose of receiving the acts;
> 4. indicate the domicile or quasi-domicile of the respondent.

(ii) The court is duty-bound to give prompt and fair attention to every petition. Specifically, the presiding judge of the court (cf. C 1425) must examine the petition to determine the competency of the court, the right of the plaintiff to plead in court, the legal and factual grounds of the petition and the correct form of the *libellus* (cf. C 1505, §§1 and 2). Within thirty days after having received the petition, the judge must issue a decree accepting or rejecting it. If no decree is issued after thirty days, the plaintiff may urge the judge to do so, and if ten more days elapse without a decree, the petition is automatically accepted by law (cf. C 1505, §3).

(iii) If the *libellus* is rejected because of a defect of form, it can be drawn up and presented again to the court (cf. C 1505, §3); if it is rejected for some other reason, the rejection can be appealed in accordance with C 1505, §4.

(b) *The Summons to the Respondent*

(i) The judicial decree accepting the petition should include a summons to the respondent to reply to the petition either in writing or orally. The summons, however, is not required if the litigants have in fact appeared before the court to pursue the case; the notary should draw up a documentary record of the appearance of the parties to respond (cf. C 1507). In any case, it is the duty of the judge to notify the respondent *at once* concerning the decree accepting the petition and the alleged grounds of nullity (cf. C 1508, §§ 1 and 2). If the respondent fails to appear, the case is tried *in absentia* (cf. CC 1592–1593). The promoter of justice (if the case demands his presence) and the defender of the bond should receive the same notification, and failure to notify them may render all subsequent acts null (cf. C 1433).

(ii) If the respondent is a minor or is insane, the summons is served to the person who should legally act in the name of this person (cf. CC 1508, §1, and 1478–1479).

(iii) The summons or citation should be served in accordance with CC 1509–1511. Once lawfully served, it produces some very important procedural effects, namely, the emergence of the *instantia* or formal suit. When a suit is said to exist, a special relationship is formed between the parties among themselves and with the court: the matter under judgment becomes subject to the laws of the suit, the jurisdiction of the court over the case is made firm, and the matter under judgment cannot be changed (cf. C 1512). This situation created by the emergence of the *instantia* continues until the definitive sentence is pronounced (cf. C 1517); the *instantia*, however, can be suspended (cf. CC 1518–1519), it can abate (cf. CC 1520–1523), and it can be renounced (CC 1524–1525), and in all these cases, the special procedural relation of the formal suit ceases to exist.

We should remember, however, that matrimonial cases, and especially those concerning nullity, are of public interest, and even if the parties may lose interest in pursuing the case, the promoter of justice may be obliged to pursue the suit in order to obtain a legal declaration concerning the validity or invalidity of a particular marriage (cf. CC 1674, §2, and 1430–1431).

(c) *The "litiscontestatio" or "Joinder" of the Issue*

C 1677

§1. When the *libellus* has been accepted, the presiding judge or the *ponens* is to proceed to the communication of the decree of citation according to the norms of can. 1508.

§2. Unless either party has petitioned for a session on the joinder of the issues (*constestatio litis*), when fifteen days have passed after such a communication, the presiding judge or the *ponens* is to determine the formulation of the doubt or doubts within ten days by a decree ex officio and notify the parties.

§3. The formulation of the doubt not only is to ask whether there is proof of nullity of marriage in the case, but it also must determine on what ground or grounds the validity of the marriage is to be challenged.

§4. Ten days after the communication of the decree, the presiding judge or the *ponens* is to arrange for the instruction of the case by a new decree if the parties were not opposed.

(i) As explicitly stated by this canon, the presiding judge or the *ponens* has ten days to formulate the terms of the case, which he does by taking into account what is being petitioned in the *libellus* and what is being replied by the respondent. The judge (or the *ponens*) formulates the *dubium*, or terms of the case, in a judicial decree that is notified to the parties. In this formulation he should specify the grounds of nullity to be subject to proof and eventual judgment (cf. C 1677, §3). The parties, then have *ten more days* to object to the formulation of the doubt. After the ten days have elapsed, a judicial decree is issued ordering the inception of the new stage of the process or presentation of *proofs*.

(2) *Second Stage: Presentation and Examination of Proofs*

The second stage of the process starts with the decree of the judge ordering the presentation of proofs (cf. C 1516). It closes with another decree, after all proofs have been collected, declaring the conclusion of the case or *conclusio in causa* (cf. C 1599). The importance of this state of the process is obvious, for the decision of the judge depends on his moral certitude concerning the matter under judgment, and if he cannot be certain, the judge must pronounce that the right claimed by the plaintiff has not been proved and cannot be legally declared. Furthermore, in matrimonial cases the validity of marriage enjoys the favor of the law and if nullity is not proved, the denial of the petition of nullity amounts to a declaration in favor of the validity of marriage.

The judge acquires moral certainty solely from the proof presented. Proof is defined by canonists as "the demonstration of the existence of a fact or of the truth of an assertion." Any kind of proof can be brought to the case, but in order to guide the judge to evaluate them, the Code established certain principles to be observed.

Principles Concerning Proofs in General:

(i) The *burden of proof* rests upon the person who asserts, whether plaintiff or respondent. In matrimonial cases, which are of public interest, the judge may also undertake the burden of proof for the sake of a morally certain and just sentence (cf. C 1600).

(ii) What needs to be proved are the *facts* that are asserted. However, a fact that is denied can also be proved indirectly if it is shown that by the circumstances of time or place something did not exist or could not have happened.

(iii) The following need not be proved:

—What the law already presumes, for instance, internal matrimonial consent is presumed to exist by its external manifestation (cf. C 1101).

—Facts admitted by both parties; however, if these facts affect the validity of marriage, they still require proof, for this is the very object of the controversy which must be resolved independently of the agreement of the parties (cf. C 1526).

(iv) Although all kinds of proof can be presented, the judge should speedily decide, after hearing the parties, which proofs are useful and licit and which ones should be rejected (cf. C 1527).

(v) The refusal of one party or a witness to appear in court to testify can be remedied by obtaining legitimate declarations outside the court (cf. C 1528).

(vi) Although for the sake of the order of the process, proofs should not be gathered before or after this stage of the process, for a *grave cause* and for the sake of a just decision, the judge can accept proofs at other times (cf. CC 1529, 1598, §2, and 1600).

Principles Concerning Some Particular Proofs:

(i) *Deposition of the Consorts*

In matrimonial cases, the testimony of the consorts is of special importance to prove the facts of the case, for the consorts generally have a direct knowledge of the facts which must be evaluated. The deposition of the consorts, therefore, should take first place after the joinder of the issue (cf. C 1530).

This deposition is to be taken by the judge, his delegate, or an "auditor" under the judge's instructions (cf. C 1428). The parties, the promoter of justice, if he intervenes, and the defender of the bond can prepare questions on which the party should be examined (cf. C 1533).

The consorts are to be examined separately. Each should provide proper *identification* before being allowed to make the depositions, unless this identification has already been sufficiently established (cf. C 1552). The judge, or the person taking his place should administer *an oath* to speak the truth from each party before the examination, or after it to confirm the truth of the testimony (cf. C 1532). If a party should refuse to take an oath, the judge may waive it, but the notary should mention this in the testimony as well as the reason for the refusal (cf. C 1568). A testimony given under oath by a person of known integrity has greater probative value than the testimony given without the oath; the reason given for the refusal to take the oath should be taken into consideration when the testimony is evaluated. The person taking the oath should be properly instructed concerning the moral and legal consequences of perjury (cf. C 1368). In the examination of each of the consorts, the following should be observed:

C 1678

§1. The defender of the bond, the advocates of the parties and the promoter of justice, if intervening in the suit, have the right:

1° to be present at the examination of the parties, the witnesses and the experts, with due regard for the prescription of can. 1559;

2° to inspect the judicial acts even though not published and to review the documents produced by the parties.

§2. The parties cannot assist at the examination mentioned in §1, n. 1.

The defender of the bond and the promoter of justice, if he or she intervenes, always retains the right to be present at the depositions of the parties, witnesses, and experts, and to inspect the judicial acts and documents; the advocates can be barred from being present at those depositions and from inspecting parts of the acts and documents when the judge decides that the process must be carried out in *secret* (cf. C 1559).

When these persons are present at the examination, they can propose to the person leading the inquiry that some questions be asked, but they should not ask the question to the party under examination, for they are not conducting the inquiry (cf. C 1561).

The consorts must be examined separately and one consort is not allowed to be present at the deposition of the other. If the depositions of the consorts disagree on facts which are of importance for the judgment of the case, the judge can later bring the consorts together or have them come to an agreement concerning the facts (cf. C 1560, §2). The judge, however, should be careful not to give occasion to collusion where the parties agree to false testimony to obtain a declaration of nullity.

The questions should not be communicated to the parties ahead of time, unless particular matters may require that the person interrogated may have time and other aids to recall the facts (cf. C 1565). The questions should be brief, accommodated to the understanding of the person interrogated, not including several points, not captious, not crafty, not leading, not offensive, and relevant to the case (cf. C 1564).

A party legitimately interrogated must answer and tell the truth. If the party refuses to answer all or some of the questions, the judge should take this refusal into account when evaluating the proof of the facts. A party, however, may interpose an exception against the questioning of the judge if it did not fulfill the requirements of C 1564.

While making their depositions, or apart from them, the consorts may *assert something against themselves.* This is called a confession which has a certain value in the evaluation of the facts, as we shall see below. A confession can be "judicial" or "extra-judicial." There is judicial confession when it is made before a judge spontaneously or upon interrogation (cf. C 1535); there is extra-judicial confession when the assertion against oneself is not made in the above mentioned circumstances.

The depositions of the parties and the confessions, whether judicial or extra-judicial have indeed a probative value, but not complete probative force can be attributed to them unless other elements thoroughly corroborate them. In order to evaluate these proofs, the law establishes a very general principal as follows:

C 1679

Unless full proofs are present from other sources, in evaluating the depositions of the parties in accord with can. 1536, the judge is to use witnesses regarding the credibility of the parties, if possible, as well as other indications and aids.

The probative value of these depositions and confessions is very diverse depending on the trustworthiness of the parties, the time when the statements were made, the source of the information concerning the facts, their agreement or disagreement with documents, other testimonies, etc. Court decisions on other cases supply a rich source of criteria for the evaluation of these testimonies in which all possible circumstances must be taken into account. These declarations and confessions have no probative value if they were made through error of fact or were extorted by force or grave fear (cf. CC 1536 and 1538).

(ii) *Proof by Documents*

Every canonical process accepts documents as proof of the facts that must be judged (cf. C 1539). A "document" is the record of a fact: A picture, a tape, a film, a writing or anything else is a document if it records a fact. Documents are *public* when authorized by competent authority and in accordance to law; they can be public *ecclesiastical* documents or public *civil* documents. All other documents that are not public are called *private* (cf. C 1541). Public documents possess full probative value about all that is directly and principally asserted unless the contrary is proved by other means (cf. C 1541). Private documents in matrimonial cases do not have full probative value: the fact should be corroborated by other proofs (cf. C 1542). If the document, whether private or public, has been erased, corrected, interpolated, or affected by any such defect, the judge should assess its probative value if any (cf. C 1542).

For any document to be assessed by the judge, it must be deposited with the chancery of the court. Only originals or authenticated copies should be accepted (cf. C 1544). A party may ask the judge to order the presentation of a document that is in possession of the other party; if the document is *common* to both parties (testament, contract among the parties, document on conjugal separation, etc.), the judge can order its exhibit in the process unless the possessor fears infamy, danger of vexation, or other serious inconvenience from its exhibition. If this should be the case, the judge may order only the partial exhibition of the document (cf. CC 1545–1546).

(iii) *Proof by Witness*

Proof by witness is admitted in every kind of process. All persons can be witnesses, except the following:

Those who are *in fact* and ordinarily incapable of an objective appraisal of the facts: those under fourteen years of age and the feeble-minded. The judge should evaluate this factual incapacity and decree that they may be heard.

Those made incapable *by law*, namely, the parties, their "patrons," the judge, the assistants to the judge and to the parties in the case, priests on anything heard with occasion of confession (cf. CC 1549–1550).

Witnesses must tell the truth, but they may not answer in matters known by reason of sacred ministry or professional secret, or if they fear infamy, dangerous vexation or other serious inconveniences (cf. C 1548).

The parties can present or reject witnesses, but it is left to the decision of the judge to determine those who must be heard (cf. CC 1551, 1553, 1555) even those not proposed by the parties (cf. C 1452). Witnesses should be called and examined by the court in accordance with CC 1551–1571. Their testimonies must be duly recorded by the notary and after proper additions, deletions, and corrections, the acts must be signed by the witness, the judge, and the notary (cf. CC 1567–1570).

For the proper evaluation of testimonies, the judge should consider the condition and reputation of the witnesses, the source of their knowledge, the consistency and certainty of the testimony, the corroboration of other witnesses and other proofs. The deposition of a single witness does not constitute full proof; other circumstances must support the testimony. One of these circumstances may be that the witness, acting in official capacity, makes a deposition regarding duties performed *ex officio* (e.g., a pastor testifying about the administration of a baptism, the assistance to a wedding, etc.) (cf. C 1573); the accuracy of this deposition can always be challenged by the presentation of contrary proof.

(iv) *Proof by Experts*

C 1680

In cases of impotence or defect of consent due to mental illness, the judge is to use the services of one or more experts unless it is obvious from the circumstances that this would be useless; in other cases the prescription of can. 1574 is to be observed.

As commonly defined, "An expert is someone who possesses specialized knowledge concerning certain facts bearing upon the issue under judgment." In cases of impotence and lack of consent due to psychic incapacity, the use of the expert is mandatory, unless the facts are so evident that no special expertise is required.

The expert who must show proof as prescribed by this canon is a consultant to the judge. This expert is designated by the judge (cf. CC 1575–1576) and acts under the direction of the judge (cf. CC 1577–1578) and his role is different from that of the expert which a party may designate (cf. C 1581) to help the party interpret the facts of the case; the private experts may also be allowed to present their opinion to the judge.

The judge must *evaluate* the proof submitted by the expert in two ways: he must examine how the expert reached the conclusions submitted and must ponder the legal consequences of the facts. The expert is not a judge of the legal case, but since the expert submits facts, the judge must explain in a decision the reasons for accepting or rejecting the facts presented by the expert (cf. CC 1578–1579), for those facts are submitted as proof and it is incumbent on the judge to reason about the proofs.

(v) *Presumptions*

A presumption is a "probable inference about an uncertain matter" (cf. C 1584). It is not a proof strictly speaking but an assessment of the facts which the proofs supply. Presumptions can be "legal" or *iuris* when the law establishes them, e.g., internal consent is presumed to conform to the words (cf. C 1101); they can be "personal" or *hominis* when the conjecture is formulated by the judge.

A legal presumption relieves the party from proof and transfers the burden of contrary proof upon the party that denies what is presumed, e.g., internal consent did not in fact conform to the words employed.

The judge must also use his own personal presumptions from particular facts that are certain and directly related to the object of the controversy, but he cannot formulate general presumptions relieving the party from the burden of proving the fact that is being asserted (cf. C 1586).

(b) *Publication of the Acts*

All proofs received in the court must be shown to the parties, except for those proofs and acts which, for the *gravest* reason must remain secret (cf. CC 1455, 1457, 1546, 1559, 1602). The judge must harmonize the need of avoiding harm resulting from the violation of a secret with the right of the parties to know all that is needed to defend their case (cf. CC 1598, §1).

The parties can present additional proofs and counter-proofs and the judge must again show these to the other party (cf. C 1598, §2).

(c) *The Conclusion of the Case*

After the parties have no further proof to present, or when the time for presentation of proofs has elapsed, or when the judge declares that he has sufficient proofs, the judge proceeds to issue a decree declaring the conclusion of the case *(conclusio in causa)*.

The case, however, should be suspended at any time during the presentation of proofs (or even after) for the following reason:

C 1681

During the instruction of a case, whenever a very probable doubt emerges that the marriage was not consummated, after suspending the nullity case with the consent of the parties, the tribunal can complete the instruction of the case for a dispensation *super rato* and then submit the acts to the Apostolic See together with a petition from either one or from both spouses for a dispensation and with the opinion of the tribunal and the bishop.

Notice that the consent of the parties is required for the process to be turned from a declaration of nullity to a petition for *dispensation of non-consummated marriage*. If the parties consent, a change of competency takes place, the process becomes administrative instead of judicial, and the court that has heard the process until now takes the role of simply gathering the proofs ("instruction" of the process) which are then sent to the Congregation for the Sacraments as prescribed in the above-quoted canon.

(3) *Third Stage:*

(a) *Discussion of the Case*

With the *conclusion* of the case, the time for presentation of proofs is closed. The judge then sets the date for the presentation of the defense briefs (cf. C 1601). Exceptionally the judge may accept further proof if he thinks it to be necessary for the just decision of the case (cf. C 1600). If the parties do not meet the deadline or simply forego their right, the judge should still hear the defender of the bond and the promoter of justice before the pronouncement of the sentence.

If the parties wish to avail themselves of defense briefs, they may present these in writing; if the judge permits it, the defense may be presented orally (cf. C 1602, §1), in which case the oral presentation should be recorded and notarized (cf. C 1605).

The defense briefs are exchanged among the parties who can then present their corresponding "replies," normally only once unless the judge for grave reason grants them the right to reply a second time. The promoter of justice and the defender of the bond can always reply twice to the defense briefs (cf. C 1603).

In order to clarify some of the matters contained in the written defense replies, a short oral discussion may be allowed (cf. C 1604).

(b) *Pronouncement of the Sentence*

A "definitive" sentence is the legal pronouncement by which the judge decides a judicial case; an "interlocutory" sentence is the pronouncement that settles incidental questions (cf. C 1607). Questions that are incidental to the principal question and must be settled before the principal question, are examined by the court by way of a contentious oral process of its own (cf. CC 1655–1670), by an abbreviated process and subsequent *decree,* or together with the principal case and its definitive sentence (cf. CC 1587–1591).

In order to pronounce any sentence, the judge must have *moral certitude* about the matter to be decided. This certitude is to be derived from the acts and proofs of the process, which the judge must evaluate in conscience and in accordance with what the law specifies about the value of some proofs. If the judge is unable to reach this certitude, he must pronounce in favor of the validity of marriage (cf. C 1608).

At the date and time set by the presiding judge, the judges meet in session where each present their report from their written conclusions. A moderate discussion follows and a decision is reached by majority vote. The sentence upon which the majority agree, is written by the relator (cf. CC 1609–1610).

Apart from other formal requirements (cf. C 1612) the sentence must resolve the controversy as formulated by the terms of the *dubium,* deciding no less than what is formulated in the doubt. Since the sentence is indeed a judgment, the legal and factual reasons on which the decision is based should be explained in the writing of the sentence (cf. C 1611).

(c) *Publication of the Sentence*

The publication of the sentence must be done as soon as possible. It consists of the fact of delivering it to the parties or their "patrons" (cf. CC 1614–1615).

Appeal Against the Sentence

(1) An appeal is a formal request to the superior court against the sentence of the lower court made by the party aggrieved by the sentence, the defender of the bond or the promoter of justice.

As a general rule, a sentence issued at the first grade of a trial *(prima instantia)* may be appealed and the case tried anew at the second grade *(secunda instantia)* by the appeal court. If the second sentence should overturn the first sentence, it can be appealed once again and the case tried at a third grade *(tertia instantia)* by the superior court. When *two conforming sentences* have been issued, no further appeal is permitted unless "new and grave reasons" are adduced (cf. C 1644). Any sentence at any grade of the trial may also be impugned by the "complaint of nullity against the sentence" (cf. CC 1619–1627), but this form of redress is quite different from the appeal which consists of an ordinary and new judgment on the controversy on no other grounds than the claim that the previous sentence has failed to protect the lawful interest of the aggrieved party or the public interest.

(2) In cases of marriage nullity, the appeal is regulated by the general rules of the ordinary contentious process contained in CC 1628–1640, except in what follows:

C 1682

§1. The sentence which first declared the nullity of the marriage together with the appeals if there are any and the other acts of the trial, are to be sent ex officio to the appellate tribunal within twenty days from the publication of the sentence.

§2. If the sentence rendered in favor of the nullity of marriage was in the first grade of trial, the appellate tribunal by its own decree is to confirm the decision without delay or admit the case to an ordinary examination of a new grade of trial, after considering the observations of the defender of the bond and those of the parties if there are any.

This canon explicitly regulates the special procedure to be followed when a sentence declares *for the first time* the *nullity of marriage,* whether this is done in the sentence issued at the "first instance" or at the "second instance" of the trial. This special procedure consists of the following: (a) all proceedings are remitted *ex officio* from the court issuing the sentence to the superior court; (b) the superior court hears the arguments, if any, of the defender of the bond and of the parties; (c) without trying the case again, the superior court *reviews* the case; (d) the court, then, proceeds without delay to decide by *decree* either to *confirm* the sentence of nullity *or to hear the case anew* according to the ordinary procedures of the appeal trial (cf. C 1640). This decree should explain the legal and factual motives for the decision (cf. C 1611, n. 3; Response from the commission for the interpretation of the Second Vatican Council decrees of February 14, 1974, *Acta Apostolicae Sedis* 6, p. 463).

(3) When the prescriptions of this canon are contrasted with the general rules of appeal contained in CC 1628–1640, the following outline can be drawn:

(a) The *first declaration of nullity*, whether at the first or at the second "instance," is always remitted *ex officio* to the superior court, which *reviews* it by a *summary process* or hears the case anew according to the ordinary appeal process;

(b) The *first sentence upholding the validity* of marriage, whether issued at the first or the second "instance," may be appealed and the case may be tried again by the superior court according to the ordinary appeal process;

(c) Two *conforming decisions*, whether both be for validity or for nullity, make the matter definitely adjudged and the sentence ready for its execution unless the special appeal foreseen by C 1644 is introduced.

(4) A special and further *appeal against two conforming* sentences, whether for nullity or for validity, may be accepted and heard at a third "instance" if "new and serious" reasons are adduced (cf. C 1644). Before opening the case anew, the court of the third "instance" must examine whether or not the reasons adduced are "new and serious" and then it must decide by decree to admit or not admit the new case.

In addition, it should be kept in mind that the same marriage may always be impugned under a *new chapter of nullity*, but this is not properly speaking an appeal but a new case even when heard by an appeal court.

(5) The *ordinary appeal process* is outlined by CC 1628–1640 as follows:

(a) The appeal against the sentence should be *filed*, within fifteen days of having received notice of its publication, with the court that issued the sentence (cf. C 1630). This court is known as the court *a quo*, or court "from which" the sentence is appealed. The filing of the appeal suspends the execution of the sentence (cf. C 1638).

(b) The appeal is *pursued* within a month of its filing before the superior court (cf. C 1633), known as court *ad quem*, or court "to which" the sentence is appealed.

(c) The right to appeal can be waived or it may abate (cf. CC 1635–1636), in which cases the sentence becomes firm and enters the stage of its execution.

(d) The appeal is pursued with a formal request similar to the bill of complaint of C 1504 attaching the appealed sentence to it (cf. C 1634). The other party may also join the appeal against the whole or any part of the same sentence (cf. C 1637).

(e) If the appeal impugns the marriage, a new chapter of nullity may be introduced as prescribed by the following canon:

C 1683

If at the appellate level a new ground of nullity of the marriage is offered, the tribunal can admit it and judge it as if in first instance.

The prescriptions of this canon are an exception to the general rule that on appeal the object of the controversy is not to be changed (cf. C 1634, §1). In matrimonial cases, the introduction of a new chapter of nullity does change the object of the controversy, and this is permitted not only on appeal but even during the trial for grave cause and with the permission of the judge (cf. C 1514).

The introduction of a new chapter of nullity does not seem possible, however, when the sentence is remitted for special *review* to the superior court (cf. C 1682), since this review consists of a *summary process*, and a new chapter of nullity would require an ordinary appeal trial.

(f) The ordinary appeal trial follows the procedures of the ordinary contentious trial with all due adaptations (cf. C 1640). The appeal trial is not a mere review of previous proceedings but a new judgment of the case *ex novo et integro*.

Execution of the Sentence

When there are two conforming sentences declaring the nullity of the marriage, the sentence is firm and can be executed. Normally, the court will add to the sentence, or to the decree confirming the nullity, an additional decree ordering its execution.

From the sentence thus completed, some effects follow as stated in the next two canons:

C 1684

§1. After the sentence which first declared the nullity of marriage has been confirmed at the appellate level either by decree or by another sentence, those persons whose marriage was declared null can contract new marriages immediately after the decree or the second sentence has been made known to them unless a prohibition is attached to this sentence or decree, or it is prohibited by a determination of the local ordinary.

§2. The prescriptions of C 1644 must be observed, even if the sentence which declared the nullity of marriage was not confirmed by another sentence but by a decree.

After the second sentence of nullity has been notified to the parties, these acquire the right to contract a new marriage (cf. C 1085). The court, however, may forbid the celebration of a new marriage for the following reasons:

(1) Reasons of procedural law: When the special appeal "for new and grave reasons" of C 1614 has been filed and the court deems that the appeal has a probable foundation, the court may forbid the marriage until the appeal is resolved in order to avoid that "irreparable damage" may be caused by the execution of the sentence (cf. CC 1644 and 1650, §3).

(2) Reasons of substantive law: When the ordinary, in accordance with C 1077, vetoes a new marriage or when the court that issued the sentence of nullity for reasons of temporal or permanent incapacity to marry (e.g., impotence or incapacity to consent) vetoes any further marriage while the impediment or the incapacity remains.

C 1685

Immediately after the sentence has been executed, the judicial vicar must notify the ordinary of the place in which the marriage was celebrated about this. He must take care that notation be made quickly in the matrimonial and baptismal registers concerning the nullity of the marriage and any prohibitions which may have been determined.

15

THE DOCUMENTARY PROCESS FOR THE DECLARATION OF MARRIAGE NULLITY

(Code of Canon Law, Book VII, CC 1686–1688)

Cases to be Tried by this Process

(1) Cases declaring the nullity of marriage are often difficult and their resolution often requires detailed procedures that guarantee a just decision. At other times, however, the nullity of a marriage can be proven by a document that is certain and unimpeachable; in these cases, the procedures that declare the nullity of marriage can be simplified as outlined in the following canon:

C 1686

When a petition has been received in accord with can. 1677, the judicial vicar or a judge designated by him, omitting the formalities of the ordinary process but having cited the parties and with the intervention of the defender of the bond, can declare the nullity of a marriage by a sentence, if from a document which is subject to no contradiction or exception there is certain proof of the existence of a diriment impediment or a defect of legitimate form, provided that it is clear with equal certitude that a dispensation was not granted; this can also be done if there is certain proof of the defect of a valid mandate of procurator.

(2) This canon prescribes a *summary process* to be followed only in the following cases: (a) Cases of nullity resulting from a *diriment impediment* that was not dispensed, or from a *substantial defect of the canonical form*, or from *lack of lawful delegation* in marriages contracted by proxy. Excluded from this process are those cases of nullity resulting from defect of consent even if this might be proved by document. (b) When

those sources of nullity can be proved by a *certain and unimpeachable document*. This document may be *public*, whether *ecclesiastical* or *civil*, as well as *private* (cf. C 1540); it may be presented in the original or in a certified copy (cf. C 1544).

The Competent Forum

(1) As stated in the canon quoted above, these cases may be heard before a *one-judge* court. The judge may be the judicial vicar or a judge designated by him from those appointed by the bishop (cf. C 1421).

(2) Since this is a judicial process, the rules of competency of C 1673 should be observed.

Development of the Summary Process

(1) *Initial stage:* The process is initiated by a *petition*, as in the ordinary process (cf. C 1502). If the petition is accepted by the judge, he issues a *summons to the respondent* in accordance with C 1508, unless the respondent has already appeared before the court (cf. C 1507, §3). If the respondent fails to appear, the case can be tried *in absentia* (cf. C 1592–1593); next, the judge proceeds to *formulate the doubt* (cf. C 1513).

(2) *Second stage:* At this stage, only one mandatory and very reasonable step should be observed: the parties, the defender of the bond and the promoter of justice (if the law requires his intervention), should be summoned and heard.

(a) The *document* that gives rise to this summary process should show with *certitude* that marriage was invalidly contracted; mere indications or probable conjecture are not sufficient to give certitude as would be the case, for instance, when documentary proof is limited to the depositions of the parties, or to the deposition of one witness, or to a private document, which never constitute full proof but require corroboration (cf. CC 1536, §2; 1542; 1573). If the document lacks certitude, the case cannot be decided through this summary process.

The canon, furthermore, requires that the document should be *beyond any well-founded suspicion* of being false or forged. The respondent and the defender of the bond may present objections and exceptions to the document, but it is up to the judge to determine, after hearing their arguments, if the document remains unimpugnable (cf. C 1543).

(b) In order to establish more firmly the truth of the documentary proof, the judge should acquire moral certitude that *no dispensation* from the impediment or from the requirement of canonical form was granted, or that *no convalidation* of marriage took place (cf. CC 1156–1165). Since this requires proof of a negative fact, and a complete investigation that the fact has not occurred is practically impossible, all that the judge should do is to establish moral certitude by means of some investigation of the baptismal and marriage records of the parties, interrogation of witnesses, and the examination of other proofs that may be available. However, if there is some indication that dispensation or convalidation may have taken place, the investigation should be pursued more thoroughly until moral certitude is attained.

(3) *The pronouncement of the sentence:* After evaluating the probative force of the document, the judge should issue the sentence declaring either the nullity of marriage or that the nullity has not been proved. He then proceeds to the publication of the decision (cf. CC 1607–1617).

Appeal

C 1687

§1. If the defender of the bond prudently thinks that either the flaws mentioned in can. 1686 or the lack of a dispensation are not certain, the defender of the bond must appeal against this declaration to the judge of second instance, to whom the acts must be sent and who must be advised in writing that it is a question of a documentary process.

§2. The party who feels aggrieved retains the right to appeal.

(1) In contrast with C 1682, in the documentary process there is no mandatory review of a sentence declaring the nullity of marriage for the first time. In this process, the first sentence declaring the nullity of marriage can be appealed only by the initiative of the parties or the defender of the bond. This is only logical if we understand that the documentary proof should be so evident that it may be accurately appraised by a summary process with no further need of review. At the same time, the law commands the defender of the bond to appeal if he esteems that the proof supporting the sentence of nullity does not meet the requirements of certitude demanded by the canon. The parties, of course, retain the right to appeal the sentence whether this be for nullity or for validity.

(2) When the sentence is appealed, the proceedings are sent to the court of the "second instance," which hears the case anew by means of the same *summary process* as described in the following canon:

C 1688

The judge in second instance with the intervention of the defender of the bond, having heard the parties, shall decree in the same way as in can. 1686 whether the sentence is to be confirmed or whether the case must be rather handled according to the ordinary process of law; and in that case the judge remands it to the tribunal of first instance.

If the judge of the "second instance" confirms the declaration of nullity, the sentence becomes firm and ready for its execution. A further appeal can be introduced only if "new and serious proofs or reasons" are adduced (cf. C 1644). If the judge of the "second instance" decides against the first sentence, the matter is remitted by decree to the court of the "first instance" for trial in accordance with the ordinary process. This decree cannot be appealed.

General Norms Governing All Processes for Declaring Marriage Nullity

These norms are given in the last three canons which regulate the processes for the declaration of nullity of marriage. Since we have already studied the principles contained in these canons, we now quote them for the convenience of the reader without any further commentary.

C 1689

In the sentence the parties are to be advised of the moral and even civil obligations which they may have to each other and to their children as regards the support and education of the latter.

C 1690

Cases declaring the nullity of marriage cannot be treated in an oral contentious process.

C 1691

In other procedural matters, the canons on trials in general and on the ordinary contentious trial are to be applied unless the nature of the matter precludes it; however, the special norms on cases involving the status of persons and affecting the public good are to be observed.

16

PROCESSES FOR THE SEPARATION
OF CONSORTS

(Code of Canon Law, Book VII, CC 1692–1696 and 1656–1670)

Legal Separation

(1) Spouses have the obligation and the right to live together in conjugal life unless excused by legitimate cause (cf. C 1151). This "life together" *(convictum)* is a particular but very important aspect of the partnership or community of life *(communitas)* which the spouses contract in marriage. For valid reasons the consorts may suspend cohabitation, either temporarily or permanently, but their physical separation for reasons of work, illness, or other such motive, does not suspend their community of life which should remain intact in other respects. The suspension of cohabitation, therefore, is different from that other situation, sanctioned by law and known as *legal separation,* which suspends the rights and obligations concerning their community of life. The causes of legal separation are contained in CC 1151–1155.

(2) Since the community of life of the spouses is the direct object of an irrevocable marriage covenant, the spouses do not have a free disposition over the rights and obligations that make up this community of life; the suspension, therefore, of these rights and obligations must be brought to the judgment of the Church. As the new Code regulates even more closely (cf. C 1152, §3) this anomalous situation of marriage, it has become urgent to educate Catholic couples about their obligation to seek the authorization of the local bishop before agreeing to a separation. Even when legal separation can be put into effect on the authority of the offended party (cf. CC 1152–1153), it cannot be protracted for

more than six months without obtaining authorization from the competent ecclesiastical authority (cf. C 1152, §3).

Jurisdiction of the Church over Cases of Separation

C 1692

§1. Personal separation of baptized spouses, unless otherwise legally provided for in particular places, can be decided by a decree of a diocesan bishop, or by a sentence of a judge in accord with the following canons.

§2. Where an ecclesiastical decision has no civil effects, or if it is foreseen that a civil sentence is not contrary to divine law, the bishop of the diocese of residence of the spouses can give them permission to approach the civil forum, having considered the particular circumstances.

§3. Also, if a case is concerned only with merely civil effects of marriage, the judge can determine it is sufficient that the case be deferred to the civil forum from the start, with due regard for the prescription of §2.

(1) The authorization to separate is an *act of jurisdiction* reserved to the diocesan bishop, and those acting in his name, to be granted in accordance with the law. Neither pastors, nor priests, nor those employed by diocesan agencies as marriage counselors or other such capacities, may authorize the separation of the spouses, not even temporarily, under the guise of pastoral or professional counselling.

(2) While acknowledging the force of particular ecclesiastical laws for some territories, this canon determines the manner by which the *ecclesiastical authority* may grant authorization to separate:

(a) The *local ordinary* by means of an *administrative process* may decree the separation. This decree, if granted, should include all necessary provisions for the support and education of the children (cf. C 1154). Against the decree of the local ordinary, the parties may use the administrative recourse foreseen by CC 1732–1739.

The resolution of these cases by administrative process before the bishop or his delegate has the advantage of allowing the use of all pastoral means to restore harmony and avoiding, as far as possible, the confrontation of the consorts in a lawsuit.

(b) The *judicial vicar* or a lawfully designated judge of the diocesan tribunal may also decide on these cases by means of a *judicial* process which may follow either the procedures of the ordinary process or those of the oral process (cf. C 1693, §1).

(3) If the decisions of the ecclesiastical authority are not recognized by the civil law, the local bishop may authorize the consorts to present their separation cases to a *civil court*, but this authorization should never

be granted if it is foreseeable that the civil court will decide in a manner that is contrary to divine law. As the legislation of the States favors divorce rather than separation, by not providing sufficient protection to the legitimate interests of the parties seeking only a separation, the recourse to the civil courts raises grave pastoral and moral problems.

It is true that a controversy over the "merely civil effects" of marriage which may derive from a canonical separation, should be in theory of the exclusive competency of the civil courts. In practice, it is not possible to bring the case to a civil court and effectively separate the "merely civil effects" from the suspension of "common conjugal life" which is of the exclusive competence of the Church. The question, therefore, of allowing cases of separation to be decided by a civil court raises moral, pastoral, and legal questions which need be resolved by the local bishop or by the Episcopal Conference.

Administrative and Judicial Procedures

C 1693

§1. Unless one party or the promoter of justice seeks an ordinary contentious process, an oral contentious process is to be used.

§2. If the ordinary contentious process has been used and an appeal is proposed, the appellate tribunal is to proceed in accord with the norm of can. 1682, §2 while observing everything that is to be observed.

(1) As said above (cf. C 1692), a petition requesting separation can be presented to the local bishop, who may hear the case *administratively* by himself or by his delegate.

(2) The bishop may decide that the case be heard *judicially* by the judicial vicar or a judge of the tribunal. In this case, as well as in the case when the petition is directly filed with the diocesan tribunal, the matter is to be resolved according to the procedures of the *oral process*. The words of C 1693 seems to indicate that the oral process is to be preferred, unless one of the parties requests the procedures of the ordinary process.

Development of the Judicial Oral Process

The *oral process* is an innovation of the new Code of Canon Law which regulates it in CC 1656–1670. It consists of a procedure before a one-judge court to decide controversies both with speed and with due regard for the rights of the parties (cf. C 1670). It cannot be used, however, when the law explicitly forbids it, as in the cases of marriage nullity (cf.

C 1669). The oral process, as it refers to cases of separation, may be outlined as follows:

(1) *Initial stage of the process:* The steps included within this stage are the same as those of the ordinary contentious process, for these steps are always necessary in judicial processes to establish the terms of the controversy. These steps are: the *petition* presented to the court which, in addition to the requirements of C 1504, should include the facts and the documents upon which the petition is based or the request to the judge to gather the proofs not accessible to the petitioner (cf. C 1658). Having examined and accepted the petition, the judge proceeds to *summon* the respondent (cf. C 1659); if the respondent should interpose any exception to be countered by the petitioner, the judge should give the petitioner some time to respond (cf. C 1660). The judge, then, proceeds to *the formulation of the doubt,* or terms of the case and to summon the parties, their patrons, the promoter of justice (cf. C 1696), the witnesses, and the experts (if needed), to a hearing (cf. C 1661).

(2) *Second stage:* This second stage consists of a hearing, or audience, where all concerned are present. The session begins with the introduction of all *exceptions and incidental actions* (cf. CC 1662; 1459–1664); then the *proofs* are presented; the depositions of the parties and the testimony of witnesses and experts are conducted by the judge during this session (cf. CC 1663–1665); if more than one session is required to complete the presentation of the proofs, the judge may decide to adjourn the hearing to another day (cf. C 1666). After the proofs are presented, the *matter is discussed* under the direction of the judge (cf. C 1667).

(3) *Third stage:* After the conclusion of the hearing, the judge may take some time for *deliberation,* or if the difficulty of the case requires it, he may summon the parties to another session within fifteen days. After proper deliberation, the judge *pronounces his decision* in the presence of the parties. The *publication of the decision* takes place when the decision is issued in writing within fifteen days from its pronouncement (cf. C 1668).

(4) *The appeal:* The appeal case from a *decision issued by the oral process* follows the ordinary contentious process with all due adaptations (cf. C 1670). If the appeal is *from a sentence issued by the ordinary process,* the case is *reviewed* by the superior court by means of the summary process prescribed by C 1682, §2. From this review the superior court may decide to confirm the first sentence by decree or to hear the case anew according to the ordinary appeal trial (cf. CC 1628–1640).

The Competent Forum

C 1694

The prescriptions of can. 1673 are to be observed in regard to the competence of the tribunal.

(1) This canon refers to the competency of the court when the case of separation is to follow the judicial process. As the canon states, the competency of the court is to be determined by the "titles" of territorial competency contained in C 1673.

(2) If the case is to be heard by the local bishop through an *administrative process*, the rules of C 1673 do not apply, for the administrative process is a more flexible procedure which should be adapted to the circumstances of the persons involved. It would seem, therefore, that the rules of domicile are sufficient to determine the competency of the local bishop over the case (cf. CC 1692, §2; 104, and 102, §1).

Reconciliation to be Attempted by the Court

C 1695

Before accepting the case and whenever it is perceived that there is hope of a successful outcome, the judge is to use pastoral means to reconcile the spouses and induce them to restore conjugal living.

(1) Recourse to pastoral means of reconciliation before accepting the case is urged again by this canon. The canon refers explicitly to the judge who is asked to hear the case judicially, but the same obligation affects the bishop or his delegate if the case is to be heard administratively.

(2) It is to be noted that the attempts at reconciliation and the restoration of common life should not be confused with attempts at arbitration and compromise, for the rights and duties that derive from the community of life are not, as we have explained, at the free disposition of the parties and cannot be subject to arbitration or compromise (cf. CC 1696 and 1715). The spouses could not, for example, legally demand a salary for his or her services to the family, or settle to condone an adulterous relationship, or renounce legally the conjugal *debitum*, and so forth. This does not mean, however, that the parties should not compromise in other forms of behavior which do not affect the strict rights and obligations that make up the conjugal common life.

(3) If the judge in his attempts at reconciliation refers the couple to a "marriage counselor" or to some other expert, he is not referring them to arbitration nor is he in any way delegating his jurisdiction which by

law cannot be delegated (cf. C 135, §3); the marriage counselor or family expert, therefore, should attempt nothing but to achieve reconciliation.

The Promoter of Justice

C 1696

Cases involving the separation of spouses also pertain to the public good; therefore, the promoter of justice must always intervene at them in accord with the norm of can. 1433.

Cases of separation of consorts are of public interest. The promoter of justice, therefore, must always intervene in these cases and his absence from the process, if he was not lawfully summoned, renders the decision invalid in accordance with C 1433.

17

PROCEDURE FOR THE DISSOLUTION OF A RATIFIED AND NON-CONSUMMATED MARRIAGE

(Code of Canon Law, Book VII, CC 1697–1706)*

Nature of this Process

"A ratified and consummated marriage cannot be dissolved by any human power or for any reason other than death" (cf. C 1141). But "a non-consummated marriage between baptized persons or between a baptized party and a non-baptized party can be dissolved by the Roman Pontiff for a just cause, at the request of both parties or of one of the parties, even if the other party is unwilling" (cf. C 1142).

The canonical process to petition the dissolution of such a marriage is outlined in CC 1697–1706. What is being asked in this petition and process is a dissolution of the bond. This is the meaning of the term "dispensation" used by the Code at the heading of this chapter and in the words of these canons. What is being asked is not a declaration of nullity, for the marriage is ratified and valid by the sole force of the marriage consent, but a true dissolution of the bond which only the Roman Pontiff may grant for a just cause.

Since what is being asked is the "grace of dispensation" and not the vindication of a right or the declaration of a fact due in justice, this process

---

*In the exposition of this procedure and of the procedure in the presumed death of a spouse, we are substantially following the commentaries of Dr. Leon del Amo and Dr. Joaquin Calvo in *Código de Derecho Canónico*, EUNSA, Pamplona (Spain) 1983.

is, most appropriately, an *administrative process*, though the services of judicial officials may be used for the gathering of proofs.

Right to Petition the Dispensation

C 1697

Only the spouses or either one, even if the other is not willing, have the right to petition for the favor of a dispensation from a ratified and not consummated marriage.

As can be seen, this canon states in terms of procedural law what is stated as a general principle of substantial law in C 1142 quoted above.

The Competent Forum

C 1698

§1. The Apostolic See alone adjudicates the fact of the non-consummation of marriage and of the existence of a just cause for granting the dispensation.

§2. The dispensation, however, is granted by the Roman Pontiff alone.

(1) The Sacred Congregation for the Sacraments to the exclusion of any other ecclesiastical authority judges (a) about the *fact of non-consummation* which must be understood in accordance with C 1061, §1, and (b) about the existence of the *just cause*, that is to say, a cause which, all things considered, should be grave enough to warrant the dissolution of the marriage bond. What may be grave in one particular case may not be grave, nor just, in another case.

(2) The dispensation, or dissolution of the bond is granted only by the authority of the Roman Pontiff.

The Petition

C 1699

§1. The person competent to accept the *libellus* seeking a dispensation is the diocesan bishop of the domicile or quasi-domicile of the petitioner, who must arrange for the instruction of the process if he is sure of the basis of the pleas.

§2. But if the proposed case has special difficulties of the juridical or moral order the diocesan bishop is to consult the Apostolic See.

§3. Recourse is open to the Apostolic See against a decree by which a bishop rejects a *libellus*.

(1) The petition is *addressed* to the Roman Pontiff, but it is *received* by the diocesan bishop. The rules of competency of C 1673 do not apply

in these cases; the bishop of the domicile or quasi-domicile of the petitioner should receive the petition.

(2) The *written* petition should contain a full and exact exposition of the facts concerning non-consummation, and should specify the just cause that motivates the petition.

(3) The bishop, by himself or by his delegate, should examine if the petition is legally well founded, consulting, if necessary, with the Sacred Congregation for the Sacraments. He, then, decides to open the process or to reject the petition. Against the decree of rejection, the party may appeal to the Sacred Congregation for the Sacraments.

(4) Following the general principle stated in C 1676, it is to be understood that the bishop should attempt reconciliation insofar as possible.

The "Instructing" Judge, The Defender of the Bond, and the "Legal Expert"

C 1700

§1. With due regard for the prescription of can. 1681, the bishop is to commit the instruction of these processes, either permanently or in individual cases, to his own tribunal, the tribunal of another diocese, or a suitable priest.

§2. But if a judicial petition has been introduced to declare the nullity of this same marriage the instruction is to be committed to the same tribunal.

The preparation of the proofs, or "instruction" of the process, may be entrusted by the bishop to the following courts or persons:

(1) When the case was initiated with a petition of nullity and a very probable doubt subsequently arises concerning the non-consummation of the marriage, the court which started hearing the case may suspend the nullity process and proceed to the instruction of the new process, as prescribed by C 1681.

(2) When the case has been initiated as a petition of dissolution of *ratum et non-consummatom*, the bishop may entrust the "instruction" of the process to his own tribunal, to that of another diocese, or to any priest well versed on these processes.

(3) When the case has been initiated with a petition of nullity to the competent court and subsequently a petition of dissolution is presented to the bishop, the "instruction" of the case of dissolution must be entrusted by the bishop who received the petition to the court that has jurisdiction over the nullity case. This is different from the case of probable doubt concerning non-consummation, for here we have a new petition about a new question presented to the bishop of the petitioner's domicile, who

may or may not be the bishop of the dioceses where the nullity case was initiated.

C 1701

§1. The defender of the bond must always intervene in these procedures.

§2. An advocate is not admitted but, because of the difficulties of a case, the bishop can permit that the petitioner or the respondent have the aid of a legal expert.

(1) Without the intervention of the defender of the bond, the acts of the process are null (cf. C 1433) and the bishop is not to remit the proceedings to the Sacred Congregation of the Sacraments without having remedied this deficiency.

(2) As the canon indicates, no advocate or procurator is admitted to the case, but the ordinary on his own initiative or at the request of the parties may allow the cooperation of a law expert. The role of this expert is not to argue for the rights of the party, for here there are no rights to defend but a grace that is requested; furthermore, since the diocesan tribunal or the priest delegated to the case (cf. C 1700) are not to judge the case but only to present the facts to the Congregation, a personal "patron" for the party is not strictly required.

"Instruction" of the Process and Publication of the Acts

C 1702

Insofar as it is possible, each spouse is to be heard during the instruction of the case; and the canons on the collection of proofs in ordinary contentious trials and in cases of marital nullity are to be observed provided they can be reconciled with the distinctive character of these processes.

(1) For the "instruction" of the process, the following practical norms should be followed in those things not derogated by the new Code: the *Rules* of the decree *Catholica doctrina* of May 7, 1923, the Instruction *Dispensationis matrimonii* of March 7, 1972; *Normae* of March 27, 1929; and the Instructions *Quo facilius* of June 10, 1935 and *Instructionem quo* of August 13, 1953.

(2) Here are some general principles concerning the preparation of these cases: (a) It is the role of the "instructing" judge to prove the *fact of "non-consummation"* and the existence of a just and proportionately grave *cause for the granting of the grace.* (b) The judge should reject *proofs* that are non-pertinent, irrelevant, or superfluous. (c) The parties and the defender of the bond must contribute to discovering the truth

for the good of the parties themselves, the public interest, and the rightful defense of the marriage bond. (d) The *depositions of the parties* have primary importance due to the intimate nature of the matter itself and because, most times, only the parties can indicate if other persons could testify concerning the fact of non-consummation. (e) These depositions should be supported by testimonies concerning the credibility of the parties and by other witnesses who can corroborate the depositions. If these witnesses are above suspicion, have testified under oath, and their testimony is consistent and in agreement with other proofs, there could be sufficient proof and moral certainty; the testimony of experts may also shed light on the causes and on the fact of non-consummation. (f) Physical examination is to be made, for it often resolves many doubts, unless it appears that it would be useless. (g) Documentary proof may include, besides an authenticated marriage certificate, letters written by the consorts to each other or to others. (h) Concerning inferences and presumptions, the causes for non-consummation and the circumstances surrounding conjugal life may be of special value to establish the facts.

C 1703

§1. There is no publication of the acts; however, when the judge sees that from the proofs introduced a grave obstacle has arisen to the petition of the plaintiff or an exception of the respondent, he is to reveal this prudently to the interested party.

§2. The judge can show to the interested party seeking it a document introduced or testimony received and set a time within which to offer observations.

(1) Although the acts that comprise all documents and proofs of the "instruction" are not to be shown to the parties, the judge must in fact show any document, testimony, or other proof which may seriously hinder either party's interest in the case, so that this party may present counterproofs or other pertinent deductions.

It would seem that the judge may allow the law experts assigned to the parties to examine the acts and suggest anything needed to complete the investigation, clarify some points, resolve inconsistencies or clear up any grave obstacle to the granting of the petition.

(2) At this point, the defender of the bond should examine the acts and write his report which should first be concerned with whether or not the appropriate procedures have been observed, and secondly on the merits of the case at hand. If as a consequence of these observations the judge should summon the parties again to resolve any inconsistency or to supply what might be missing, the defender of the bond should also be heard again before closing the case.

The Opinion of the Bishop

C 1704

§1. Having finished the instruction, the judge instructor is to hand over all the acts with an appropriate report to the bishop, who is to prepare his opinion on the truth of the matter both concerning the fact of non-consummation, and the just cause for a dispensation and the opportuneness of the favor.

§2. If the instruction of the process has been committed to another tribunal in accord with can. 1700, the observations in favor of the bond are to be made in the same forum, but the opinion mentioned in §1 pertains to the bishop committing it, to whom the instructor is to forward the acts with an appropriate report.

(1) As explained before, the final decision of the case and the granting of the grace is reserved to the Roman Pontiff after the judgment of the Sacred Congregation for the Sacraments. The local bishop, however, is asked to give his own judgment concerning the fact of non-consummation, the just cause, and on the opportunity of granting the grace. The bishop may use the expert knowledge of another person in preparing the "opinion," but ultimately he must make it his own.

This opinion of the bishop is different from the report, or *relatio* of the "instructing" judge. The latter should favor neither marriage nor its dissolution; he should report the facts of the case clearly to help the bishop write his opinion knowingly and freely.

(2) All the acts of the "instruction," the observation of the defender of the bond, and the judge's *relatio* are sent to the bishop who ordered the process, even when he made use of another diocese's court and corresponding defender of the bond.

Judgment of the Sacred Congregation for the Sacraments

C 1705

§1. The bishop is to send to the Apostolic See all the acts with his opinion and the observations of the defender of the bond.

§2. If, in the judgment of the Apostolic See, a supplement to the instruction is required, the bishop will be informed about the point on which the instruction must be completed.

§3. But, if the Apostolic See responds that non-consummation has not been established from the proofs, then the legal expert mentioned in can. 1701, §2, can review the acts of the process but not the opinion of the bishop, at the tribunal, to see whether any serious reasons warrant resubmitting the petition.

(1) The bishop should send all proceedings together with his own opinion to the Sacred Congregation for the Sacraments. The Congregation may ask for further information on the case specifying what is required; the bishop then remits this request to the court or person who "instructed" the case for its completion.

(2) If the Sacred Congregation for the Sacraments should decide that the fact of non-consummation has not been proved, the law expert of the parties may examine the copy of the acts kept in the court that "instructed" the case, except for the opinion of the bishop. Having examined the acts, the law expert may present again the petition to the court if he can adduce some "grave reasons" not considered before.

The Granting of the Grace and its Execution

C 1706

The rescript of dispensation is sent to the bishop by the Apostolic See; he shall notify the parties about the rescript and also as soon as possible order the pastor of the place where the marriage was contracted and the pastor of the place of baptism to note the granted dispensation in the registers of marriage and of baptism.

(1) The granting of the grace produces its effects from the moment in which the papal decree is issued; it is not valid, however, if the marriage has been consummated before the grace was granted, or if the alleged just cause was false.

(2) Upon receiving the decree of dispensation, the bishop should immediately notify the parties and their pastors about it, as prescribed by the canon. The pontifical dispensation, however, may contain a *prohibition* to contract a new marriage. The prohibition, can be of two kinds: (a) If the fact of non-consummation is due to lesser causes, the prohibition can be removed by the local bishop if the person is in fact able to take up his or her marriage obligations and promises to fulfill them in the future. (b) If the fact of non-consummation is due to grave physical or psychic defects, the prohibition can be removed only by the Sacred Congregation of the Sacraments if it is shown that the person is able to perform the conjugal act. In any case, the prohibition to contract a new marriage is not diriment if not explicitly stated in the rescript (cf. Instruction *Dispensationis, Acta Apostolicae Sedis* 64 [1972] pp. 244–252).

18

PROCEDURE IN PRESUMED DEATH OF A SPOUSE

(Code of Canon Law, Book VII, C 1707)

C 1707

§1. Whenever the death of a spouse cannot be proven by an authentic ecclesiastical or civil document, the other spouse is not considered free from the bond of marriage until after a declaration of presumed death is made by the diocesan bishop.

§2. The diocesan bishop can make the declaration mentioned in §1 only after appropriate investigations have enabled him to attain moral certitude of the death of a spouse from the depositions of witnesses, from rumor, or from indications. The mere absence of a spouse even for a long time, is insufficient.

§3. The bishop is to consult the Apostolic See about uncertain and complex cases.

(1) An authentic document, whether civil or ecclesiastical, certifying the death of the spouse is sufficient proof that the surviving spouse is free to enter a new marriage; the pastor can authorize the new marriage if there is no other obstacle.

(2) If there is no authentic death certificate, a new marriage cannot be contracted until the doubt is resolved and it becomes morally certain that the marriage is dissolved by death of one of the consorts. This is the logical consequence of the principle of indissolubility of marriage and of the legal presumption that marriage enjoys the favor of the law (cf. C 1060). In canon law, therefore, the absence or disappearance of one of the consorts never constitutes presumption of death. Rather, the death of the consort must be proved and moral certitude must be acquired before the other consort may be free to marry again.

(3) In order to acquire this moral certitude, a procedure must be initiated with the diocesan bishop.

(a) This procedure is initiated by a *petition* addressed to the bishop who may delegate the gathering of the proofs to his tribunal or to another apt person.

(b) The canon does not explicitly require the intervention of the promoter of justice or the defender of the bond, but since these are cases that concern the public interest, the intervention of the promoter of justice may be required by the nature of the matter (cf. C 1431).

(c) The investigation about the presumed fact of the spouse's death should use all ordinary legal proofs: deposition under oath of the surviving consort, publication of notices concerning disappearance, testimonies of witnesses, if any, concerning the death or other circumstances, documents, conjectures, rumors, and all other indications.

(4) It is incumbent on the bishop to judge the proofs of the investigation. If the bishop reaches moral certitude concerning the spouse's death, he issues a *decree* of presumed death. If the case remains doubtful or very complicated, the bishop is to consult with the Sacred Congregation for the Sacraments. If the bishop should not accept the petition or should deny the declaration of presumed death, the petitioner may appeal to the Sacred Congregation for the Sacraments.

PART III

MARRIAGE NULLITY ON GROUNDS OF CONSENSUAL INCAPACITY

Canon 1095 and Its Application by Judicial Process

Rev. Ignatius Gramunt, J. Lic., J.C.D.
Prof. Leroy A. Wauck, Ph.D.

INTRODUCTION

By its very nature matrimony consists of a legal relationship between a man and a woman regarding definite rights and obligations. Matrimony, however, is not the exclusive province of the law and of legal studies, and both civil and ecclesiastical law have acknowledged their dependence on other disciplines, for it has always been evident that marriage consent and marriage life, being typically human and rational acts, are the proper object of the study of psychology (philosophical and empirical), and present day canonists are fond of speaking of married life as an "interpersonal relationship" with rich psychological implications. More importantly, the theological dimension of marriage colors every aspect of this legal relationship. In fact, the competence which the Church claims over the marriage between Christians and its regulation and study by canon law is due to its sacramental nature. Marriage, therefore, is also the proper object of study of Theology and of pastoral practice.

The theological and psychological dimensions of marriage have been rightly emphasized in recent times to avoid impoverishing its significance because of a narrow and legalistic mentality, but as often happens with any interdisciplinary study, the diversity of methods proper to each discipline can contribute to obscure the discussion rather than enlighten it. Of all the canons on matrimony, perhaps C 1095 is the one which best illustrates the ambiguities which can obscure any interdisciplinary study.

Another difficulty, more practical perhaps than theoretical, derives from the equivocal use of the term "pastoral." Being pastoral means leading the faithful (*suaviter et fortiter*) to accommodate their conduct to the principles of Christian life, while accommodating the law to fit the vagaries of human conduct may be expedient but is not pastoral. When expediency prevails, even the praiseworthy desire of bringing back to the sacraments those who are invalidly married leads to interpretations that are contrary to the law's pastoral intent (cf. John Paul II, Apostolic Constitution *Familiaris Consortio*, n. 84, November 22, 1981).

163

In the first part of this study, we shall try to understand the legal rule of consensual incapacity to contract marriage. In the second part we will study the application of this rule to particular marriages impugned before an ecclesiastical court. Hopefully we may also come to a better understanding of marriage consent, the key legal element of the marriage contract, a most typically human and rational act, and the efficient cause of the sacrament (cf. S.Th.Supl. q.45, a.l, ad prim.).

One final introductory note: On February 5, 1987, John Paul II provided an authentic interpretation of C 1095 in his address to the Roman Rota (cf. *L'Osservatore Romano*, Feb. 5, 1987). Although our commentary on this canon in the next two chapters was written before the Pope's address, it conforms to the Holy Father's interpretation of both the substantial and procedural law concerning "psychic incapacity" to contract marriage.

19

THE LEGAL RULE OF CONSENSUAL INCAPACITY

Consensual Incapacity as formulated by C 1095

Matrimonial consent is the essence of the matrimonial contract and the juridic act that produces marriage. The Code dedicates a separate chapter to the conditions under which this juridic act produces, or fails to produce, a marriage contract, and the very first condition is that it should be a human act endowed with that psychological integrity which makes it a true and free choice.

This first requirement is established by C 1095 which formulates a consensual incapacity deriving from a psychological defect. The Code does not define consensual "capacity" for marriage but only consensual "incapacity." This may be due to the legislative technique of using negative precepts, which being restrictive, are more practical—a technique used in all other canons of the same chapter. But the negative definition of "incapacity" suggests something of greater importance: every adult person is *presumed to possess* sufficient psychological capacity for marriage, and only those persons who are afflicted by some psychological defect, as defined by C 1095, are incapable of contracting marriage.

The cause of the consensual incapacity defined by C 1095 is a psychological defect or disorder. The legislator, however, does not define the disorder using the technical terms of clinical psychology or psychiatry for, apart from the difficulties inherent in these classifications, the legislator is here interested in describing the psychological disorder by its effect on the integrity of the juridic act from which the marriage contract derives. From this follows an important and practical consequence: not every psychological defect incapacitates a person for marriage, but only that defect or disorder which affects the integrity of consent. Canonists prefer to speak of "consensual incapacity" rather than psychological incapacity, for although the cause of the incapacity is indeed psychological, the canon formulates it as incapacity for matrimonial consent, the key juridic act which produces marriage.

Another point that needs to be made in this connection, is that this incapacity does not constitute a legal impediment and, in fact, it is not included among the impediments in chapter III. Impediments are *prohibitions* which render a person legally incapable of a valid marriage, while consensual incapacity, as formulated by C 1095, is not a prohibition but a most *radical inability* to establish marriage due to the lack of sufficient consent, the one juridic act which can produce marriage. An obvious consequence of what we have just stated is that a pastor (or his delegate) cannot prohibit marriage to those afflicted by a psychological disorder even if he suspects that there might be a case of consensual incapacity. At the most, and following the general principles of moral theology, he can refuse to assist at a marriage celebration only when the person intending marriage is *manifestly* incapable of receiving the sacraments. But beyond these cases the pastor has no legal power to prohibit marriage to anyone who is of age and otherwise not affected by an impediment (C 1058), one of the prohibitions which require the intervention of the ordinary (cf. CC 1071, 1077 and 1120) or by a judicial decree explicitly forbidding a person to enter a new marriage when the previous marriage has been declared null on grounds of consensual incapacity (cf. CC 1077, 1419, §1 and 1420, §1 and 2).

Capacity (or incapacity) always makes reference to an object to be apprehended and which is the measure of that capacity. In our case, the object is marriage, and more specifically, the essential rights and obligations which make up that "partnership of the whole of life" (cf. C 1055) which we call marriage. If these rights and obligations are included in the act of consent, this consent produces marriage; if not, consent is defective and fails to produce marriage. If by some defect in the rational faculties, a person is not capable of apprehending these rights and obligations and of including them in the act of consent, we have a case of consensual incapacity due to a psychological defect. According to C 1095, this consensual incapacity is produced when a person, (1) lacks sufficient use of reason; (2) labors under a grave defect of discretion, (3) is psychologically unable to assume the essential obligations of marriage.

In the normal course of events, a person after puberty reaches that stage of psychological and physical development in which one is naturally prepared to seek a partner in life among persons of the opposite sex in order to raise a family, and this partnership is sought as one, exclusive and unbreakable. Nature itself inclines a person to this object for which no other psychosomatic capacity is required than that which is attained after the development of puberty is completed. The person, therefore, who after that age is not capable of apprehending and fulfilling these essential rights and obligations is affected by a psychological defect which incapacitates this person for a valid matrimonial consent. A person may be ignorant or in error about *some* of the essential rights and obligations of marriage and this ignorance or error may indeed vitiate consent, but the incapacity we are studying is one caused by a defect or lack of integration of the rational faculties incapacitating a person to sufficiently apprehend the essential rights and obligations of marriage and arrive at an act of consent that is psychologically complete and sufficient.

The Psychology of Marriage Consent

Consent is an act of the will approving of a choice, and choice, to use Aristotle's definition, is "a desire proceeding from counsel" (cf. S.Th.I,q.83,a.3); that is to say, an act of the will that results from the deliberation of the intellect concerning the value of an object or situation. In scholastics terms a choice is a *practical judgment* formed by an act of the will leading the intellect to consider the motives of the choice, while the will is itself determined by the intellect to choose here and now in accordance with the perceived motives.

As the scholastic axiom reminds us, *nihil volitum nisi precognitum:* The appetitive powers depend on the cognitive powers and nothing, indeed, can be willed if it is not previously known. In fact, in every rational act, intellect and will work conjointly with each other and with the sensory powers, for both intellect and will depend for their proper operations on the information supplied by the external senses and processed by the internal senses (perception, imagination, memory, cogitative power). The senses, at the same time, receive their cognitive and appetitive force from being united to the rational powers of the soul, the underlying principle of all human operations. In the formation of a choice (or practical judgment), the *vis cogitativa* or particular reason plays a crucial role, for it is the particular function of this internal sense to perceive the usefulness or harmfulness of a particular object. This assessment does not determine the rational faculties, but it serves them in presenting to them a particular object under the aspect of usefulness. In this joint and harmonic cooperation of the rational and sensory powers, the act of consent consummates the psychological activity of the soul in its quest to capture reality and to be united with it.

In the case of matrimonial consent, the *practical judgment* that forms the choice of the will is a judgment about the desirability here and now of establishing a lifelong partnership with a particular person for the purpose of mutual help and offspring. This is not a speculative judgment about the utility or goodness of marriage in general, its nature and properties, but a judgment formed with the intervention of the will leading the intellect to judge about the desirability of this marriage here and now to this particular person, while the will is simultaneously determined by the same judgment to choose accordingly. At the same time, the desirability of a particular marriage is dependent, as we have stated before, on the *vis cogitativa* or particular reason, that power of human sensory activity whose function is to grasp the "utility" of a particular object as satisfying one's needs.

The *deliberation* that forms this practical judgment requires a speculative judgment about the essential elements and properties of marriage, but a speculative judgment by itself has no efficacious power to move the will to make a specific choice or determination. Unless the will moves the intellect to a judgment of desirability towards an object perceived as desirable by particular reason (or *vis cogitativa*) there cannot be a genuine choice on the part of the will. Matrimonial consent, therefore, can take place only when the sensory and rational powers intervene to form a practical judgment of the intellect concerning the good of a particular marriage. Since the *vis cogitativa* belongs to the order of physical senses, we can easily see that its function in forming a marriage consent cannot properly begin to operate before puberty, for the interior senses are also dependent on the normal neuro-physiological development of the body. Marriage consent is the crowning point of all the psychological operations involved in that mutual attraction of the sexes by which nature inclines a person to marriage.

The analysis of the psychological elements that form matrimonial consent is necessary to understand but not sufficient in itself to define capacity for marriage consent, since any capacity (psychological or otherwise) has to be measured by the object which is included within this capacity. In other words, to define any kind of capacity we must answer the question, capacity for *what?* Obviously in our case, the object of this consensual capacity is marriage, an object that we must primarily define in legal terms, since marriage, as said before, is essentially though not exclusively, a legal relationship that involves the giving and accepting of very personal rights and obligations. These essential rights and obligations, which are the object of matrimonial consent are: (1) The right and obligation to a community of life and love, which is one, exclusive and indissoluble. (2) The right and obligation to mutual help and offspring, for which this community exists. (3) The right and obligation to the conjugal act as directed towards procreation (cf. CC 1055–1057).

The "community of life and love," which constitutes one of the essential rights and obligations and forms the object of sufficient consent, has been stressed by some canonists in order to bring out the interpersonal element of the marriage relationship. This phrase is taken from the Constitution *Gaudium et Spes* (n. 48) of the Second Vatican Council. Although not incorporated into the letter of the canons, the phrase is commonly accepted as very apt to define the nature of the marital relationship. It should not be interpreted, however, to imply a *near-perfect* relationship, for such a thing could not be claimed or given as a legal right or obligation. The precise meaning of this statement is to be derived from its relation to the right and duty to mutual help and to the procreation and education of offspring, for these latter goods make up the community of life and love that is the marriage relationship. At the same time "mutual help" and "the procreation and education of offspring" should be understood as goods to be claimed and given only within the "community of life and love." The need to differentiate the essential rights and obligations of marriage in order to better understand the nature of this legal relationship does not permit us to separate them as unrelated to one another, for all these rights and obligations together constitute marriage and if separated are meaningless. If one understands that nature itself inclines the person to these essential goods, after the time of puberty, we shall not interpret the term rhetorically as if only a perfect relationship could constitute a true marriage.

Capacity to consent to these essential rights and obligations requires, in the first place, the speculative knowledge (or *scientia*) that marriage is ordered to the achievement of those goods contained in the essential rights and obligations. In the second place, capacity to consent to the *same* rights and obligations requires the ability to estimate, by means of *ratio particularis*, whether or not a particular person is desirable here and now for the purpose of achieving those goods which form the essence of marriage. From the intellectual knowledge of the essential rights and obligations, and from the particular assessment of particular reason concerning the same rights and duties to be exchanged here and now with this person, a practical judgment and a choice follows concerning this particular marriage.

The capacity to form this syllogism is the ability to deliberate or critically evaluate, which is necessary to achieve valid consent with respect to a given marriage. Terms such as "deliberation" or "critical power" should not lead us to think that marital consent requires a capacity to formulate the essential rights and obligations of marriage in a highly formalized manner or the ability to deliberate in scientific fashion about them, for the speculative knowledge of the good implied in these rights and obligations—what marriage is and requires, is accessible even to the inarticulate knowledge of a child: the speculative judgment concerning the essential rights and obligations of marriage requires only the simple, ordinary use of reason. Deliberation, on the other hand, requires more than speculative knowledge, for it consists of the assessment done by particular reason, though this deliberation is nothing more than an assessment about the desirability of this particular marriage spontaneously done by the *vis cogitativa* at the time that a person has reached adulthood.

The person who lacks the necessary use of reason to make a speculative judgment about the essential rights and obligations of marriage cannot begin to elicit the proper act of consent; or a person who lacks the discretion needed to assess the same rights and obligations as particular goods desirable here and now cannot arrive at the practical judgment concerning the same rights and obligations. Furthermore, a person who cannot assume *in fact* the same essential obligations, to which everyone is by nature inclined after puberty, lacks that unity and integration of the cognitive and appetitive powers within his or her personality which are required to arrive at a practical judgment and free choice over the same essential obligations. We shall return to the discussion of these three types of defective consent after we study the age of sufficient consent.

The Age of Psychological Capacity for Sufficient Marriage Consent

Aquinas observes that as man acquires the use of reason gradually, different stages of discretion can be distinguished: the first stage covers those years before a person reaches the seventh year of age approximately. At that age a second stage begins to unfold, and as a person reaches the next stage, approximately towards the fourteenth year of age, a rapid development takes place and a person becomes able to judge and dispose of those things which pertain to his or her own person. However, in what refers to things external, a person acquires that capacity at a later stage of discretion or by the twenty-first year of age approximately (cf. S.Th. Sup.q.43, a.2).

As we have seen, mere use of reason, or capacity for speculative knowledge *(scientia)* is never sufficient to form a practical judgment, because any choice requires the intervention of that particular perception supplied by the cogitative power or particular reason. In what refers to marriage, this perception is dependent upon the psychological and physiological development that takes place during puberty.

The term "puberty" is used here not as referring only to the physiological development of sexuality: we are using the term to mean that transitional period in a person's life characterized by a number of physiological and psychological changes which modern psychology identifies as early and middle adolescence. During these years, and parallel to the physiological development of sexuality, a person begins to acquire a growing consciousness of self in relation with the world outside: the adolescent begins to ponder about his or her person and about other persons and social institutions as they relate to himself or herself. This pondering consists of a critical assessment of the world around, which shows the rise of a new and more comprehensive perception of reality. Under this new perception, a person comes to think in a reflective and more self-conscious fashion about another person of the opposite sex as a possible complement to one's life-plan and as a particular good which should fulfill one's needs.

This perception and assessment of another person of the opposite sex is the particular function of particular reason, or *vis cogitativa*. As explained before, this interior sense derives its cognitive power from its union with the intellect, but since it belongs to the order of physical senses, it depends for its operation on the appropriate physiological development. It is not difficult to see, therefore, that the physiological development which takes place at puberty is the *conditio sine qua non* for the discernment that should precede the practical judgment which is marriage consent.

Taken in its wider sense, puberty is a period of psychological development. The acquisition of new perceptions and the resulting critical judgment which develops during these years are also dependent on educational or cultural influences. Thus it may happen that in a culture which keeps the young from assuming responsibility during their teen years, their discernment concerning many aspects of life tends to be protracted. In addition, a materialistic and permissive culture which fosters an early sexual expressiveness together with a protracted adolescence, tends to retard or distort the development of a person's discernment concerning the objective value and the goods of marriage. Under those conditions the integration of the cognitive and appetitive powers within the growing personality, known as "maturation," can be frustrated and even warped.

In a normal and healthy environment, the completion of the time of puberty (in its wider meaning), is the natural stage of a person's development culminating in the capacity for marital consent. This has been universally recognized in both civil and canon law, although the determination of this fact by a well-defined legal rule is not free of some difficulties. The first difficulty is to be found in the impossibility of establishing sharply defined limits to a physiological and psycho-social development which is gradual and different in each individual person. The most that the law can do is to establish presumptions concerning the time when this process is completed in *most* individuals.

In canon law, this presumption is found in the impediment of age which, as formulated by C 1083, forbids a woman before age fourteen and a man before age sixteen to enter a valid marriage. In the legal system preceding the 1917 Code, the law presumed that puberty, and consensual capacity for marriage, was sufficiently reached by ages twelve/fourteen for women and men respectively. But even then, it was always understood that if puberty had been reached before the presumed age, a person could be dispensed from the impediment and contract a valid marriage. Regardless of the particular determination of age made by the legal presumption, the fact remains that puberty has been recognized by the law as the *age of sufficient psychological capacity* for valid marriage consent.

This is confirmed by C 1096, which presumes that by the time of puberty a person has sufficient knowledge *(scientia)* concerning the nature and purpose of the marital act and, therefore, sufficient cognitive capacity for the act of matrimonial consent. However, as we have seen, mere *scientia*, or speculative knowledge is not sufficient to provide the basis for consent, since even a child before puberty has sufficient psychological capacity to know *speculatively* about the nature and purpose of marriage. But what the canon implies is that since puberty is the time of sufficient psychosomatic development to contract marriage, it is presumed that by this time a person also has sufficient knowledge about the sexual aspect of marriage. In other words, the presumption is based upon the fact that by the age of puberty a person has acquired sufficient psychological capacity to know about the very essentials of marriage and to choose in accordance with that knowledge. The law acknowledges, therefore, that puberty is the natural age of discretion—*matrimonio proportionata*. The law, however cannot determine the exact age of puberty in calendar years except by means of a legal presumption admitting of contrary proof.

The formulation of a rule of positive law based on the natural fact of puberty encounters other difficulties. By the end of the development of puberty, a person has sufficient psychological capacity to consent to the essential rights and obligations of marriage, but at that minimal age a person often lacks the wisdom and character to resolve certain demands which, while not strictly speaking essential to marriage, nevertheless make up a healthy marriage life. Having reached a new stage of discretion, which is sufficient for matrimonial consent, a person has not yet reached the following stage when one is sufficiently capable to dispose of things external to himself. As Gasparri noted in his commentary to C 1082 of the 1917 Code, (now contained in CC 1072 and 1083, §1), the Church came to require a higher age for the validity of marriage because the necessary discretion of mind which one might have before that age (fourteen and sixteen) is still weak, and the practice of married life before that age is often harmful both to parents and children. For the same reason both the former and the present Codes attempt to dissuade minors (now those under eighteen years of age) from contracting marriage (cf. C 1071, §1, n. 6 and C 1072), and the present Code in C 1083, §2 gives to the Episcopal Conference the power to raise the age requirement of the under-age impediment for the *licit*, though not the valid, celebration of marriage. Although the formulation of the natural rule of puberty into a well-defined and practical rule of positive law presents some important pastoral difficulties, it is to be noted that all the canons cited above acknowledge, at least by implication, that puberty determines the age of discretion for marriage consent, for this is a fact of nature which positive law cannot change. Recognizing, however, that matrimonial life is not adequately protected by the sufficient but minimal discretion attained with puberty, the canons seek to keep a balance between the *ius connubii* of any person naturally capable of marriage and the prudent exercise of this right. But since puberty, in the wider sense, is the fact of nature which makes a person psychologically capable of marriage consent, the law has no other alternative than to accept this fact with its inherent ambiguity.

Contemporary psychologists speak of a late adolescence which can go as far as the twenty-fifth year for males. But at this stage of psychological development, all elements needed for mature discernment are already present. By late adolescence a person has sufficient capacity to deal with most ordinary life situations and begins to put this capacity into operation when confronted by these new situations for the first time. But since we are examining here the minimal but sufficient capacity to consent to the essential rights and obligations of marriage, we must conclude, as we have seen, that minimal but sufficient capacity arises, in the normal course of events, with the completion of the physiological and psychological development of puberty, that is to say, by middle adolescence and not later.

Matrimonial consent, as we have seen, consists of a practical judgment on the essential rights and obligations in a particular marriage. In the normal course of events, a person is psychologically capable of arriving at such a practical judgment by middle adolescence. This is a natural fact and it is the rule of positive law concerning consensual capacity. The rule of puberty cannot be defined with exactitude, but this does not make it impractical or useless for, regardless of the specific age when this development occurs in each person, puberty is a fact of nature easily recognized and the standard or measure of *capacity* to contract marriage. If this standard is neglected in the study of consensual capacity, we run the risk of seeking artificial or arbitrary standards which do not adequately explain the degree of discretion needed for valid matrimonial consent.

The Legal Rule of Consensual Incapacity

Following our discussion of consensual *capacity*, we are better prepared to understand the rule of consensual *incapacity* set forth in C 1095. This is a three-fold rule containing three types of consensual incapacity. As explained previously, the first two types exist when the inadequacy of consent derives from a deficiency of the psychological elements needed to arrive at the practical judgment that forms consent. The third type of consensual incapacity exists when consent is ineffective because of a defect in the rational powers, which makes it impossible for the subject to assume the essential obligation of marriage. Briefly we shall look at these three types:

(1) *Lack of sufficient use of reason.*

Use of reason means the ability to make judgments that correspond to reality. Obviously, a person who is not capable of such judgments even at the speculative level can hardly arrive at a practical judgment which is the basis of consent. Sufficient use of reason is normally acquired by the seventh year of age (the first stage of discretion). Not only are infants affected by this deficiency but also those adults who are afflicted by a psychological defect that prevents them from knowing what they are doing, even though they may retain some elementary perceptions. The lack of sufficient reason may be caused by a psychological disorder or by other transitory or more permanent conditions such as toxic or hypnotic states, drunkenness, somnambulism, drug-addiction, alcoholism. In all these cases, it is necessary to determine the lack of sufficient reason *at the time of giving consent,* for this is what truly invalidates the matrimonial contract, not just the fact that the disorder exists or has existed at some time.

(2) *Grave defect of "discretio iudicii."*

Due discretion or discretion of judgment consists of the ability to assess particular goods as suitable for one's needs. In what concerns the assessment of those goods contained in the essential rights and obligations of marriage, this capacity is acquired, as we have explained, by the time a person completes the maturation of puberty (the next stage of discretion). A person who labors under some disorder which prevents him or her from making a particular assessment concerning the desirability of this particular marriage (with its essential rights and obligations), cannot arrive at the practical judgment involved in matrimonial consent. This, however, is *not to be confused* with error of judgment or "poor judgment," since a *mistake* in judgment concerning the character of one's spouse or the circumstances surrounding the marriage does not mean incapacity. A person who is psychologically capable can rectify the mistakes or draw greater good from them, but a person who *lacks* the *fundamental psychological make-up* is simply not able to be committed to the "essential matrimonial rights and obligations to be given and accepted." The *grave* defect contemplated here is a defect of discretion concerning these rights and obligations which are basic goods to which one is inclined by nature by the age of puberty.

If a marriage is to be declared invalid, what must be proven is not so much the gravity of the disorder as it affects other areas of life but as it refers to the defect of judgment concerning the essential rights and obligations of marriage at the moment of giving consent, although it is usually true that such grave disorders do tend to "spill over" into many, if not all, important areas of life.

This defect of judgment may be due to some psychopathology or to what has been called simply "immaturity," a retardation of that psychological development expected by the age of puberty. It should be noted, however, that such retardation cannot remain for long without constituting in fact an abnormality that is easily identifiable by clinical psychology as a "fixation." A person might have been truly "immature" at the moment of contracting marriage but had grown into maturity with time and with marriage itself, in which case whatever defect of consent may have existed at the moment of the wedding can be healed later by a new act of consent given privately and in secret (cf. C 1159). But if the psychological development has not taken place after some reasonable time, the marriage remains null for lack of sufficient consent.

(3) *Inability to assume the essential obligations of marriage.*

A person who lacks the use of reason or sufficient discretion over the matter of the matrimonial contract cannot arrive at a practical judgment which constitutes the act of consent. But the psychological incapacity to consent can also be revealed by the *factual* impossibility to assume the matrimonial obligations which one may have consented to *in theory.* The first two incapacities are described as an insufficiency of the cognitive powers needed to arrive at a practical judgment on marriage; this third incapacity is described as a *radical* ineffectiveness of the act of consent externally manifested, the ineffectiveness being due to a psychological defect also. It has been argued among canonists as to whether or not a person can have sufficient use of reason and due discretion of judgment concerning the essential rights and obligations of marriage and be unable in fact to assume these obligations due to a lack of *internal* freedom. A first reading of C 1095 would seem to imply that the law admits such possibility. Let us remember, however, that the law formulates this incapacity from a juridic point of view, being less interested in describing the act of consent and more interested in defining the psychological disorder by its effect upon the juridic act that produces marriage. The "incapacity to assume" describes a psychological disorder which makes consent ineffective thus lacking that integrity that is necessary to the complete and sufficient act that can produce marriage. We think that the psychological disorder that incapacitates a person to assume these obligations renders the person also incapable of the practical judgment which constitutes consent. To say otherwise would imply a denial of the unity of the sensory and spiritual powers (both cognitive and appetitive) and to maintain by implication that a person can be psychologically normal and yet incapable of assuming the essential obligations of marriage. To avoid such misunderstanding, this incapacity is formulated by the law with the words "due to causes of a psychic nature."

In order to determine whether or not a particular person was incapable of contracting marriage, the following facts should be established: (a) the real impossibility of assuming the essential obligations of marriage, (b) that this impossibility was due to a psychological abnormality, (c) that the disorder did in fact exist and was operative at the time of giving consent, and was not a later development.

The psychological capacity to assume the essential rights and obligations of marriage is attained, as we have seen, with the completion of the psycho-physiological development of puberty. It is a common experience that at that age, a person is more capable than he or she ever will be for that giving of oneself in an exclusive and total community of life and love. This is not to say that with age a person loses this psychological capacity for marriage, but we wish to highlight the fact that indeed *nature itself inclines a person to marriage* (cf. S.Th. Supl. q.41, a.1), and this appears manifestly so in those early years. Since this is a natural capacity after puberty, its absence constitutes a psychological disorder. The *mere difficulty* in fulfilling these obligations, which should be overcome by ordinary effort, obviously *does not constitute incapacity*.

20

THE JUDICIAL DECLARATION OF CONSENSUAL INCAPACITY

Having studied the legal rule of consensual incapacity, we shall now discuss the canonical process for the application of this rule to those marriages impugned on grounds of consensual incapacity before an ecclesiastical court. The goal of the judicial process is to reach a decision concerning the validity or invalidity of a particular marriage. In order to reach this decision, the law prescribes that *there must be moral certitude in the mind of the judge about the matter to be settled. The judge must derive this certitude from the acts and the proofs* (cf. C 1608, §1 and 2).

The Concept of Moral Certitude

"Certitude" is defined as the state of the mind in which the mind, based upon the understanding of valid reasons, assents to a judgment without fear of error. Although certitude is indeed a subjective state of the mind, it is based upon valid reasons deriving from objective evidence, for it is in the nature of objective reality as apprehended by the mind to supply the motive for certitude.

There are, however, *degrees of certitude* depending on the intelligible force of the evidence: the firmest certitude receives the name of "metaphysical" certitude, which is based on the understanding of the metaphysical laws of being which allow for no exception, for such exception would involve an internal contradiction as in the judgment, "the whole is greater than any of its parts." The next degree of certitude is called "physical" certitude, which is based on the understanding of the physical laws, which do not admit exceptions in the ordinary course of

179

physical events as in the judgment "the sun will rise tomorrow." A weaker state of certitude, but certitude nevertheless, is "moral" certitude which is based on the understanding of the customary conduct of human beings (hence the term "moral," which is not synonymous with "ethical"). In the laws of human conduct, exceptions are possible but, to the extent that we can speak of laws of human conduct, exceptions are not to be expected in the normal course of events, and we are able to derive certitude in our judgment of human acts.

Certitude is to be distinguished from *opinion* which is the state of the mind that, assenting to the truth of a judgment, it accepts the possibility of error because the evidence does not exclude the probability that the contrary is true.

The difference between certitude and opinion depends on the force of *objective evidence*. This evidence can be internal or external. "Internal evidence" is that which derives from the understanding of the thing itself thus compelling the mind to assent; it is "direct" when the truth is apprehended directly from the object; it is "indirect" when the truth is apprehended by means of a reasoning process. I am certain that it rained yesterday because I was outdoors and got drenched (direct evidence), but I am also certain that it rained the day before because when I went out, I saw all the signs that it had rained (indirect evidence). "External evidence" is that which derives from reasons outside the thing itself and compels the mind to assent because it would be imprudent to doubt the truth of these reasons, as is the case when all weather reports assure me that it rained yesterday, although I had no perception of it.

In judicial decisions, the evidence is often external for the judge has to rely on depositions of the parties, testimonies of witnesses, the opinion of experts, and other documents that are external to the object at issue. Even though none of these proofs individually considered constitute full proof, their accumulation can constitute sufficient evidence to compel moral certitude. This is clearly expressed in the often quoted interpretation of Pius XII. The Roman Pontiff characterizes moral certitude as that which excludes a well-founded or reasonable doubt; it is different from mere probability or opinion, and different also from absolute certainty, which does not admit contrary possibility. Moral certitude is necessary and sufficient to render a judicial decision even when absolute certitude could be reached (cf. *Acta Apostolicae Sedis* 34 [1942] pp. 338–342). Complementing this teaching, John Paul II affirms that the judge must draw certitude from the acts and the proofs, and emphasizes the need to scrutinize all the proofs so that they constitute true evidence. In order to reach certitude, the Pope continues, "the judge must act with a critical sense" (cf. *Acta Apostolicae Sedis* 72 [1980] pp. 172–178; cf. Paul VI, *Acta Apostolicae Sedis* 70 [1978] pp. 181–186).

It is in the context of these philosophical terms that we can better understand the words of the canon stating that for the pronouncement of a sentence, the judge must have reached a state of moral certitude. This certitude, which must exist *in animo iudici* is a subjective state of the mind on the part of the judge, but one to be derived not from conjecture or hypothesis but from the objective evidence supplied by *the acts and the proofs*.

From all of the above, two characteristics emerge concerning *objective evidence* in judicial processes: (a) It is normally made up of many facts. (b) These facts must be carefully proved. If this is true of any judicial decision, it is specially so in cases where the judge must reach moral certitude about the existence of psychological defect, for such defect is often hidden and difficult to prove unless there is a sufficient number and competent interpretation of the facts that should supply the evidence.

The Investigation of Consent: The Role of the Expert and the Role of the Judge

The application of the law to the particular case under judgment is a jurisdictional act which belongs exclusively to the judge. In order to execute his role with responsibility, the judge must know the law as well as the legal techniques of inquiry and assessment of the facts legally relevant. In the cases we are considering, the fact to be established is the validity or invalidity of a particular act of matrimonial consent, which has been impugned on grounds of consensual incapacity as described by C 1095. Incapacity for matrimonial consent is a legal concept, that is to say, a particular determination of the law concerning a most typically human reality—the freedom of the will, which is the proper object of the specialized knowledge of psychology and its clinical branches. In determining, therefore, the legal capacity or incapacity for a particular act of matrimonial consent, the judge must turn to an expert in psychology who can assess the psychological integrity of the same act. Only then can the competent court of law determine the legal capacity of the person for a valid act of matrimonial consent.

With this in mind, we must now examine the proper role of the expert in providing the psychological facts which should enable the court to declare the law to the disputed question with moral certitude.

(1) *The Role of the Court Expert.*

An expert is someone who possesses specialized knowledge concerning certain facts bearing upon the issue under judgment. In the case we are studying, the expert is a professional psychologist or psychiatrist. Since the matter has some relevance concerning the quality of the proof supplied by the experts, we have to distinguish between the expert designated by the court and the expert designated by the parties. The first acts under the direction of the judge as a consultant of the court (cf. CC 1575–1578); the second helps the party to evaluate the facts and show proof supporting his or her claim (cf. C 1581). We are mainly interested in examining the role of the *court expert* for this expert, by his particular role, has a greater influence in forming the moral certitude of the judges. In fact, C 1680 prescribes that "in cases of impotence or defect of consent due to mental illness, the judge is to use the services of one or more experts unless it is obvious from the circumstances that this would be useless."

The role of the court expert is to determine whether or not the act of consent was affected by any psychological defect at the time it was given. In order to fulfill his or her proper role as a collaborator of the judge, the expert must (a) know the end or purpose of the examination, (b) conduct the examination according to the rules and methods of his or her specialty, and (c) report the findings and conclusions to the court.

(a) In order to give a proper assessment of the psychological integrity of the act of consent, the expert receives from the judge the appropriate instructions and particular questions to which he should respond (cf. C 1577). The expert will have a better understanding of the purpose of the examination to be conducted, if that person knows the law on matrimonial consent and incapacity. He need not be a law expert but should know that his opinion is being asked for the purpose of determining the legal effects of consent. At the same time, however, the expert should know that he is not being asked for the legal validity of consent, for this is the exclusive province of the court.

Rotal jurisprudence and canonical doctrine insist on keeping the roles of expert and judge clearly distinct and repeatedly warn the expert not to prejudge the issue in his conclusions. The expert may find this distinction difficult to maintain in actual practice, mainly when the questions posed by the judge may demand of him an opinion that is nearly legal if not totally legal. It seems to us, however, that the expert should not feel unduly restricted by these warnings: they are less directed to experts and more to the judges, for the judges, as we shall see later, should not accept the conclusions of the expert at face value but should evaluate and criticize the report of the expert keeping in mind all the facts of the case and viewing them under the light of their legal knowledge. The distinction of functions just described is important to remind the judges that they cannot base their judgment on someone else's assessment of the facts. We shall return to this question when we examine the proper role of the judge.

(b) The expert should use all the methods of examination required by the rules of his own specialty. These are: (i) *Reports, testimonies, clinical histories.* C 1577, §2 requires the judge to make the acts of the process available to the examination of the expert. Some authors hold that the expert is to examine only those acts that are necessary for the performance of his special role. As a general procedural rule referring to all kinds of experts in all types of processes, this is a very reasonable caution; when it refers, however, to the court-appointed expert in cases of consensual incapacity for marriage consent, it seems wiser to provide the expert with as much data as possible and let that expert examine all the acts of the case, unless some particular matter not related to the expert's assessment should be kept from him or her for grave reasons. (ii) *Examination of the subject, which, depending on the case, may require a physical as well as a psychological examination.* The need for a personal examination of the subject by the court-appointed expert might not be necessary and not even advisable, when another reliable expert's report already exists and the court-appointed expert is only asked to examine the existing reports. Otherwise, it would seem that the personal examination of the subject with the administration of tests and use of other appropriate methods of examination is needed, for without it, the expert's opinion may remain too tentative and the proof of the case may remain insufficient to compel moral certitude. The personal examination of the subject and the administration of tests must lead to a competent interpretation of the data collected. It goes without saying that the expert should be aware of the reliability of the tests and should be able to provide a competent interpretation of the results. Here is where the expert plays his unique and distinctive role.

(c) Moral certitude as we have seen before, is different from absolute certitude, and different also from opinion or mere probability. It must be grounded on a *sufficient* number of facts and in their *connection,* all of which must be contained in the *report.* The quality of the evidence does not depend on the number of the facts but on the relevance of the proven facts. However, a certain number of significant and proven facts, or symptoms, must be shown if a psychological disorder is to be proved. In accordance with C 1578, this report should clearly indicate the documents and other means of assessment, the method followed to appraise the facts, and the principal arguments in which the conclusions are based. The judge can summon the expert to supply further information. In other words, the competence of the study and the logic of the argument must be such as to compel certitude that excludes a prudent fear of error.

In the report the expert should attempt to describe the disorder, define its nature, development, degree of abnormal behavior, effects upon reason, discretion of judgment, and free will with a special determination of the *time* when these defects affected the person. A possible scheme of such report could run as follows: (i) An *introductory part* where the instructions of the judge, if any, are referred to and the questions presented by the judge are recorded together with a reference to the acts and other documents received for his examination; (ii) An *exposition of the facts* properly arranged according to time and other circumstances that may help explain the cause, development and effects of the disorder. Here the expert should express his or her opinion concerning the truth of these facts for they constitute the basis for any further reasoning; (iii) A *clinical history* directed to show the relation between biological and environmental circumstances (family, friends, work, marriage) and the disorder. It may be necessary to note that the more hypothetical the picture described, the lesser is its value in compelling moral certitude; (iv) *Results from the personal examination* of the subject, whether physical or psychological, and from the tests administered together with the interpretation of the same results. Here the expert should express his or her opinion concerning the reliability of tests administered and his or her degree of confidence in the other methods of assessment. (v) The *conclusions*. These should follow logically from everything said before and should constitute a summary answer to the questions asked by the judge.

Having outlined the role of the expert, we can now look into the question concerning the actual necessity of the court expert. C 1680 makes the use of the expert mandatory in cases of psychological incapacity with the exception, however, of cases where this should appear useless according to all evidence. It is up to the responsible estimation of the judge to dispense from the services of the expert in obvious cases. Apart from the obvious cases, does the court require the proof supplied by an expert when the judge is a man of training and experience in psychology? Can't the court reach moral certitude without the professional report of the expert? Neither the canon nor its interpreters can say that the expert is *absolutely* required, but the words of the law itself, the jurisprudence of the Roman Rota, and the nature of the issue seem to urge the importance of using the services of an expert independently of the particular expertise of the judge. It seems to us also that experience shows the wisdom of not confusing the roles of the expert and of the judge if the judge is to reach a decision with detachment, independence, and on sufficient objective evidence. If it is true that the expert should not play judge, it is equally true that the judge should not play psychologist.

(2) *Evaluation of the Proof by the Judge.*

The third paragraph of C 1608 states that "the judge must evaluate the proofs conscientiously with due regard for the prescriptions of the law concerning the efficacy of certain proofs"; and in relation with the probative force of the expert's conclusions, C 1579, §1 directs the judge "to weigh attentively not only the conclusions of the experts, even when they are concordant, but also the other circumstances of the case."

These two canons show, among others, that the canonical judicial process adheres to the principle of "free evaluation" of the proofs by the judge. The "due regard for the prescriptions of the law" constitutes no exception to the principle, for a reading of other canons concerning the efficacy of proofs (e.g., CC 1526, 1531, 1536–1538, 1541–1544, 1572–1573) reveals that these prescriptions are prudential norms to guide the judge in the evaluation of the proofs.

The principle of free evaluation of the proofs by the judge should not give rise to any arbitrariness on the part of the judge, for the prescriptions of the canons always direct the judge to weigh the evidence objectively and in conscience and, as explicitly required by canon 1579, §2, to show in his decision the reasons for accepting or rejecting the conclusions of the expert.

In evaluating the proof supplied by the expert, the judge should take into account both the subjective and objective elements of this proof.

(a) *The subjective element* of the proof, that is to say, the person of the expert himself. C 1576 states that an expert can be excluded or rejected for the same reasons of excluding a witness. This canon allows us to apply by analogy to the expert what is prescribed by C 1572 for the witness, namely, the direction given to the judge to evaluate the witness' credibility. Thus the judge should take into consideration the possible interest that the expert may have in his client's case, his professional competence to appraise the case, and even the school of thought of the expert, for it will be rather difficult for someone who adheres to some deterministic theories of the human psyche to appreciate the nature of free consent.

The court-appointed expert should not be exempted from this type of evaluation. Although it seems obvious that in this case the evaluation should have taken place before the appointment, a court-appointed expert with all necessary qualifications can also fail to live up to the requirements of a particular case. There is nothing derogatory intended towards the expert in this critical judgment of the court, which must be diligent in appraising everything needed to attain moral certitude in conscience in such an important issue as the validity of marriage.

(b) *The objective element* of the testimony, or the report of the expert should be carefully evaluated. In the first place, the judge should appraise the truth of the facts on which the expert bases his opinion. A competent expert should express his opinion concerning the truths of these facts, but it can easily happen that as the expert takes many of the facts from the acts of the process, he may assume them to be true, for it is not his role to conduct the "instruction" of the process. The judge should further examine that these facts are not contradicted by other proven facts. The judge should evaluate the reliability of the method of examination used by the expert, for the court is interested in facts that are *certain*. Finally, the judge should examine that the conclusions follow logically from the certain and proven facts of the report. When the facts of the report are proven, the method used in the examination is reliable, and the conclusions are drawn with logic, the judge should accept the expert's report as evidence.

As said before, the conclusions of the report should answer the questions posed by the judge. If the judge poses the right questions, the job of the expert, and the subsequent evaluation of the judge, will be greatly facilitated. These questions will necessarily vary from case to case, but fundamentally what the judge should ask and the expert should answer is: (a) Did the subject labor under any kind of psychological defect at the time of the wedding? (b) To what degree did the disorder affect the use of reason, the discretion of judgment or the freedom of the will? (c) How certain is the expert about the truth of the conclusions?

Concerning the degree of certitude, it has been observed that on the one hand, experts trained in the empirical method tend to seek physical rather than moral certitude; that is to say, they seek to explain the case according to the rules of their own specialty which, if at all possible, should admit of no exception. As we have seen, this is not the certitude which the law requires. Other experts, on the other hand, may adhere to certain theories of personality which, proposed at the speculative level, are only hypothetical although the expert may regard them as scientifically proved. Hypothesis, as said before, will provide opinion only, not moral certitude. The judge must also be on guard against the tendency to accept a merely plausible explanation of events as tantamount to certitude.

Following the evaluation of the expert's report, the court may accept or reject the evidence, either totally or partially, in accordance with the principle of free evaluation discussed above. This does not imply that the judge can arbitrarily dismiss the conclusions of the expert. In fact C 1579, §2 directs the judge to justify with sufficient reasons the rejection of the expert's conclusions. If logic and objectivity is required from the expert, it is required even more so from the court, which should base its decision on the acts and the proofs and write the sentence in a well reasoned manner (cf. C 1612, §§2 and 3).

It is obvious from what we have written that the judge should have a good grasp of the concepts, arguments, and techniques of the psychological sciences, but should the judge be in fact an expert? This is not an idle question, for how can the judge evaluate a specialized subject matter in which he is not an expert? The answer is that the judge is only required to understand the facts and evaluate the expert's report from the wider view of enlightened common sense and from the perspective of the law. From these points of view, the judge can and must evaluate the proof of the expert with prudence and with justice. It is true, however, that the ecclesiastical judge must be well trained in philosophy and theology, be an expert in the law, and have a wide knowledge of the empirical sciences. This is not an impossible task though it may be a demanding one, for such are the very high qualities required of the ecclesiastical judge.

The Judicial Decision

The evaluation of the evidence is a prerequisite for judgment. In the cases we are considering, the judgment consists of determining whether or not the psychological defect, if any, affected the act of consent in such a way as to make it legally invalid. At this stage of the process, the judge has received from the expert a certain "measure" or degree of the defect involved; now the judge must compare this measure with the legal rule, for it is obvious that not every defective human act is legally invalid as not every legally invalid act is humanly defective.

The legal rule of consensual incapacity for a valid marriage is found in the three types of incapacity contained in C 1095. This legal rule is an innovation of the new Code, which greatly helps us to understand the concept of incapacity to give consent. We may add that the new law does not require more perfection of consent than it required before the promulgation of the Code, for free consent is a requirement of natural law which cannot change. But the new legal rule does define more closely how free consent can be vitiated by some psychological defect and render a person incapable of eliciting this natural-law requirement in a valid manner. The legal rule of consensual incapacity must, of course, be well understood, for this is the very first condition to apply the law to the particular case. When the law is well understood, even in its general and abstract character, and when the concrete facts of a situation are certain, the mind spontaneously perceives whether the facts fit or do not fit within the legal rule, and the judgment is made objectively and with certitude.

The last paragraph of C 1608 establishes that "a judge who cannot arrive at this (moral) certitude is to pronounce that the right of the petitioner is not established, and is to dismiss the respondent as absolved unless there is a question of a case which enjoys the favor of the law, in which case the decision must be in favor of it." As matrimony does enjoy the favor of the law, the absence of moral certitude concerning the case of nullity obliges the judge to uphold its validity (cf. C 1060).

Moral certitude is to be found in the evidence or not to be found at all; the sentence is the judgment of the court declaring to have attained or failed to attain moral certitude concerning the "doubt" presented to the court. According to judicial custom, when the court decides against the alleged nullity, the court declares that the allegation is not proved (*non constat*), even if the sentence could declare that, based upon the evidence, it is morally certain that the marriage was validly contracted. For purpose of judicial efficiency, however, the court is not required to make such declaration: the force of the legal presumption of C 1060 is sufficient.

The canons require one more thing from the court: *to show* that the judgment is not an arbitrary one. As prescribed by C 1610, the sentence must be given in writing and must contain the reasons and motives, both in law and in fact, on which it is based (cf. CC 1611, §3 and 1622, §2). The dispositive part or command (*imperium*) of the decision must be based on a true act of reason (*iudicium*). This judgment must be well founded, well reasoned, and clearly articulated, showing why and how moral certitude has been attained or not attained. In fact, the ordinary format of a judicial decision follows the logic of a syllogism: the law, the proven facts, and the conclusions.

In the processes of marriage nullity on grounds of consensual incapacity, the key to a just outcome is to be found in the collaboration between the court and the court-appointed expert: if the law is well known, if the concept of moral certitude is well understood, and if the object of the expert's report is well defined, the court will have no great difficulties in reaching a decision that conforms both to truth and justice.

BIBLIOGRAPHY

Allers, R., "The General Psychology of Adolescence," in *Character Education in Adolescence*. New York: Joseph Wagner, 1940.

Aquinas, St. Thomas, *Summa Theologiae* I, q. 78, a. 4; q. 81, a. 3; q. 83, a. 3; q. 84, a. 6; q. 86, a. 1; I–II, q. 13, a. 2 ad 3; q. 10, a. 3 ad 3; II–II, q. 47, a. 3 ad 3; Suppl. qq. 41–49; *De Anima* lll, 1.8; *Contra Gentiles* II, 60; *De Veritate*, q. 10, a. 5; q. 22, a. 9 ad 6; q. 24, a. 1.

Belenchon, E., *La Prueba Pericial en los Procesos de Nulidad de Matrimonio*. Pamplona: EUNSA, 1982.

Bittle, C. N., *Reality and the Mind*. Milwaukee: Bruce, 1949.

Brennan, R. E., *Thomistic Psychology*. New York: Macmillan, 1946, 133–35, 144–46, 201–2, 224–26.

Burke, R. L. "Lack of Discretion of Judgement Because of Schizophrenia: Doctrine and Recent Rotal Jurisprudence. Rome: Analecta Gregoriana, 1986.

Del Amo, L., "Valoracion Juridica del Peritaje Psiquiatrico," *Ius Canonicum* 22 (1982) 651–706.

Di Felici, A., S.R.R. Decis. (14-V-84) in *Monitor Ecclesiasticus* 109 (1984-IV). S.R.R. Decis. (6-V-70) in *Monitor Ecclesiasticus* 96 (1971).

Doyle, Th. P., in *The Code of Canon Law. A Text and Commentary*. Mahwah, N.J.: Paulist Press, 1985, 775–79.

Egan, E. M., "The Nullity of Marriage for Reason of Insanity or Lack of Due Discretion," *Ephemerides Iuris Canonici* 39 (1983); "Incapacity of Assuming the Essential Obligations of Marriage," *Studia Canonica* 16 (1983) 261–67; "Incapacity of Assuming Obligations," *Studia Canonica* 18 (1984) 487–96.

Felici, P., S.R.R. Decis., vol. 49 (3-XII-1957).

Gasparri, P., *Tractatus canonicus de matrimonio. Editio nova.* Typis Polyglottis Vaticanis, 1932.

Keating, J.R., "The Province of the Law and the Province of Forensic Psychiatry in Marriage Nullity Trials," *Studia Canonica* 4 (1970) 5–23.

Lefebvre, Ch., S.R.R. Decis. (31-I-1976) *Ephemerides Iuris Canonici* 32 (1976) 287.

McMahon, H., "The Role of Psychiatric and Psychological Experts in Nullity Cases," *Studia Canonica* 9 (1975) 63–75.

Mendonca, A., "The Effect of Paranoid Personality on Matrimonial Consent," *Studia Canonica* 18 (1984), 253–89; "The Incapacity to Contract Marriage" *Studia Canonica* 19 (1985) 259–325.

Pompedda, M. F. "Ancora nevrosi episcopatie in rapporto al consenso matrimoniale," in "Borderline, nevrosi e psicopatie in riferimento al consenso matrimoniale," *Studia et Documenta Iuris Canonici* 12, Ed. Officium Libri Catholici, Rome, 1981.

Serrano, J. M. S.R.R. Decis. (9-VII–1976), *Monitor Ecclesiasticus* 102 (1977) 371.

Tejero, E., "La discrecion de juicio para consentir en matrimonio," *Ius Canonicum* 22 (1982) 403–534.

Viladrich, P., in *Codigo de Derecho Canonico. Edicion Anotada.* Pamplona: EUNSA, 1983, 654–58.

INDEX